Choosing Me Now

Kim Oliver

Third in the Inside Out Empowerment™ Series
Published by InsideOut Press
www.ChoosingMeNow.com

Cover design: Denise Daub
Interior design: Veronica Daub

ISBN-13: 978-0-9853026-7-2
First Edition
Printed in the United States of America

*T*his book is dedicated to my seven grandchildren: Saige, Zavier, Logan, Emerson, Maeson, Perry, Mallory, and those yet to come. I love you all and am intrigued, honored, and in awe watching each of you becoming the persons you are going to be. I hope you learn about *Choosing Me Now* early in your life so you will take care of and love yourselves to the moon and back.

ACKNOWLEDGEMENTS

This is the place where I get to publically thank the people who have been supportive, encouraging, and helpful during the process of creating *Choosing Me Now*. Unfortunately, to really appreciate everyone who fits this description, I'd have to write another whole book!

I'd like to start with Dr. Nancy Buck, my mentor and friend, who was the very first person to teach me the concepts of Choice Theory and Reality Therapy. Over time, she transformed from my teacher, to mentor, to friend. Whenever I was wrestling with a concept, she provided brilliant dialogue to always expand my thinking.

I wouldn't be able to write anything without acknowledging Dr. William Glasser, the author and creator of the ideas that form the foundation of all I do and teach. Choice Theory and Reality Therapy changed my life in only amazing ways. It is standing on his spiritual shoulders that I am able to communicate the words I write to others.

I am also grateful for the work of Barnes Boffey, another Choice Theory mentor, who taught me that the basic needs are something that are available to us. The basic needs are not only satisfied externally but can also be satisfied within us.

I want to thank my friends, Sharon Case and Chuck Thompson, for inviting me on their family vacation to Cabo. When I am first writing and need the information to flow effortlessly, being in a beautiful, warm, sunny remote location definitely helps. Their willingness to include me afforded me the perfect space to write.

My college roommate, maid of honor in my wedding in 1983, Darlene Mort Davario, accompanied me to Cabo and was the ever patient friend, willing to explore independently while I was writing without ever complaining about the time I spent at the computer.

I had two spiritual guides, LO'real Pinder and Ania at aniasangels.com, who both provided the vision of writing this book. Interesting they could see it before I could, but their vision encouraged me to begin my journey with this book.

I need to give a shout out to my Writer's Group who challenged me to do more than mentor them, but to also write my truth. Thanks, ladies!

I thank Pam Holtzman and Kristina Lininger for helping me mastermind the title. It definitely was a combined effort!

I also want to say thank you to Marcus Gentry who helped me refine some of my early material by lending his patient ear and brilliant expertise.

When it came time for peer review, I called on my trusted and respected Choice Theory colleagues who painstakingly helped me hone each chapter of this book: Terri Allen, Suzi Hollock-Bannigan, Sylvester Baugh, Maggie Bolton, Anna Corbett, Ellen Gélinas, Carleen Glasser, Susan Mease Graham, Vanessa White Fernandez, Pam Holtzman, Cindy Knapp, Dr. Lois Dasilva-Knapton, Cindy Knapp, Jenny Lundak, Zahra Khoshnevisan, Jan Moré, Jill Morris, Clare Ong, Patricia Robey, Lynn Sumida, Shruti Tekwani, and Lee Anna Simons.

I'd also like to thank the experts in the field who helped me hone my chapters: Crystal Alston, Richard Doss, Sue Elliott, Conchetta Jones, Felicia Houston, Karen O'Donnell, Lissa Elliott StClair, Doranita Tyler, and Kate Webster.

I want to thank Denise Daub for designing this wonderful cover and my Facebook friends for helping me choose the image to be used.

I am so grateful to Veronica Daub, who did such a kick ass job on editing this book. The delight I experienced reading her edits made the editing process genuinely fun.

And I want to thank my team for their unbending support of my work – Denise Daub, Crystal Alston, Shruti Tekwani and Jennifer Stoner. I couldn't what I do without you.

And finally, I want to thank my family—my father for telling me there were no limits to what I could do, my mother for her unfailing support, and my wonderful sons and their families who provide the motivation for the work that I do.

CONTENTS

CHOOSING ME NOW

THE JOURNEY BEGINS . . .

"Journey within yourself. Enter a mine of rubies and bathe in the splendor of your own light. O great one, Journey from self to Self and find the mine of gold. Leave behind what is sour and bitter. Move toward what is sweet."
– Rumi

I dedicate the existence of this book to those people in my life who consistently told me to "take care of myself." Some of these people were close, some strangers, and some casual acquaintances, but I'm not sure what they saw in me that I didn't see in myself. I was happy, had meaningful work, and only supportive relationships in my life. What more did I need?

I had to admit, loving and taking care of myself sounded right; it's easy to hear the truth in it. So, I would say, "Okay, I will," before turning around and continuing exactly as I had been. It's not because I didn't want to care for myself nor that I failed to see the value in it, but simply because I didn't have a clear picture of what that looked like.

What does it mean to take care of yourself? How does one do that? I'm a master at taking care of others but, apparently, I wasn't doing a great job of taking care of myself! Thus the concept of *Choosing Me Now* was born.

In the past, I allowed myself to be hurt before I would ever do anything to hurt anyone else. I would tell myself that I am strong and could handle pain, fear, and disappointment. I would give to others before giving to myself; for instance, I loaned people money when I couldn't pay my own bills. It's all well and good to take care of others, but not at the cost of doing less for yourself. Caring for yourself first and using the surplus to care for others is the new formula I am implementing in my life.

Some people already know this universal truth. It's not just a philosophy, but something that is applied in real life. It is the idea behind the emergency procedure on an airplane in which passengers are told to put on their own oxygen mask before helping others, as they will be in a better position to do so. Without putting your wellbeing first, you can become a zombie of sorts, trying to help others when, in that state of ignoring your own physical and emotional health, you cannot help anyone.

I realized that, in order to take care of my physical and emotional health, I had to do something I had never attempted before: I had to develop a healthy, positive relationship with myself.

Just like relationships with others, I've discovered that this relationship with yourself requires energy and attention—it won't happen on its own. First, you need to get to know yourself if you don't already—what you like and what you don't—so you can decide what's working and what's not working in your life. Developing a healthy, positive relationship with yourself requires that you value yourself enough to believe you are worth caring for and then prioritizing the time to actually nurture yourself.

You may have noticed in Rumi's quote at the start of this chapter, the word Self starts with a capital "S." This refers to your highest and best Self—the one who is connected to both your environment and Spirit. Throughout this journey, you will be shifting from an ego-based self to a more enlightened Self.

This book began as my own journey in exploring how to create a healthy relationship with Self, and learning to value myself enough to start *Choosing Me Now*. While working out how to have a loving relationship with myself, I struggled with the concept and realized others must be struggling as well. If I wanted to help others, I had to discover it for myself first.

When I began to write this book, I planned for it to have

just three sections—money, health, and love. However, once I started, as so many books do, it took on a life of its own.

The first part I wrote was about your relationship with your finances; it was an area I had recently worked through and felt quite proud of. I created a system for helping others in serious debt and wanted to share it. I stayed up all night writing the first draft of that chapter and it flowed effortlessly. Then the book sat untouched for a full year, without even one word being added.

That's because I had decided my next section should be about the relationship we have with our bodies. While I knew what I needed to do to align myself in that area, I didn't want to do it, and I didn't want to write a book about what I knew people *should* do. I wanted to write a book about what I had already done, but I wasn't ready to make those changes yet.

A year later, I was driving and desperately needed to use a bathroom. The first place I stopped at wasn't open. Yikes! I drove a bit further and found an open restaurant, ran inside and used one of the stalls. It was freshly painted with only three separate messages written on the wall: *don't forget to love yourself, you are perfect in every way,* and *you are beautiful!*

I don't know about you, but I really don't believe in coincidences. I took that graffiti as a sign from the Universe that I was supposed to write this book—that there were people in the world who desperately needed and were waiting to read this information.

Then I got an invitation from a friend to go to Cabo, the same resort where I wrote my last book, *Secrets of Happy Couples.* I thought it must be another sign; I was meant to go to finish writing *Choosing Me Now.*

While I was there, with the beautiful ocean, the cliffs and the whales, I realized this book was much bigger than just finances, health, and love. I wanted to find a way to connect it to the foundation of everything I teach, Dr. William Glasser's Choice Theory® psychology.

I asked myself, How does a person create a relationship

with someone? The Choice Theory answer is that two people create a relationship by getting to know one another, and when they do, they find things that satisfy one of more of their basic needs. They then place each other in their respective Quality World, that place where we hold experiences with people, places, things, values, and ideas that have met at least or more of our basic needs.

The relationship you have with yourself works exactly the same way. You need to get to know yourself and find things you like that satisfy your basic human needs. Once I made that connection, I knew exactly how to illuminate the path to creating a healthy positive relationship with your Self by applying Choice Theory psychology.

CHOICE THEORY PSYCHOLOGY

"Life isn't about finding yourself. Life is about creating yourself."
– George Bernard Shaw

I thought about the concepts that make up Dr. William Glasser's Choice Theory, the concepts I have dedicated my life to. When I learned about Choice Theory in 1987, it was described as an explanation of human behavior. I had graduated from college with a psychology degree and was encouraged to be "eclectic." To me, this meant I knew a little about a lot of things but not a lot about anything. I worked with clients by trial and error... a little behavior modification, a little Gestalt therapy, and a little psychoanalysis thrown in for good measure. All I really did was make it up as I went along. Choice Theory provided me with a navigational system to find my way through anything a client, or anyone for that matter, would tell me.

Over time, Dr. Glasser evolved his theory from a mere explanation of human behavior to a way of living one's life that emphasizes the development of healthy relationships with the important people in our lives. He taught his followers to stop trying to control everyone around them and to start being supportive and encouraging instead.

Living according to Choice Theory principles changed my life. It helped me deal with the death of my husband, raise my two teenage boys by myself, survive my youngest son's two years in Iraq as a soldier, and navigate the recovery of a hot air balloon accident.

Choice Theory has applications for counselors and therapists, psychologists, nurses, teachers, managers, parents, couples, and anyone interested in self-growth and development. Choice Theory teaches that every single person is born with five basic human needs. Dr. Glasser called them Survival, Love & Belonging, Power, Freedom, and Fun. He taught that they are genetically programmed and we all have them, but the difference is that different needs are stronger for different people.

Throughout your life, you have experiences with people, things, places, values, and beliefs that satisfy, or that you believe will satisfy, one or more of these needs. Those things that satisfy your needs then become part of what Choice Theory calls your "Quality World." This is your ideal world as it represents how you want things to be.

Everyone has the same five basic needs; our Quality World is filled with pictures of the things we want to satisfy those needs. When you say, "I *need* a new car," what you really mean is that you *want* a new car. Perhaps that car would meet one or more of your needs, but it's there in your Quality World as something you want to better satisfy your needs.

If you were able to live in your Quality World, you would be happy and satisfied one-hundred percent of the time, but you don't get to live there. You have to live in the real world where some things match your Quality World but many things don't.

The relationship you have with yourself is created in the same way. You have a picture of your Self in your Quality World, the best possible version of you based on what's most important to you. In my Quality World, I am compassionate, funny, beautiful, and I sing like Celine Dion, among other things. Sometimes I get glimpses of that woman in the real world (except for the Celine part), but more often my perception of my real self doesn't match up with the ideal version in my Quality World.

When your perception of who you are doesn't match your ultimate version of yourself, you feel disappointed, frustrated, and maybe depressed or angry. You then tend to criticize, dislike, and possibly even feel hatred toward yourself. This is not a recipe for a loving, caring relationship—something in that equation has to change.

When I rethought the way I wanted to write this book, I decided to teach a little Choice Theory by having a section for each need. I then chose three aspects of each need that I found important in developing a good relationship with Self; there may be others you would like to create for yourself. Perhaps there will be a Volume II of *Choosing Me Now*, but for this version, what follows are the areas I chose.

For my purposes, I adjusted the names and shifted the perspective of some of the needs. Choice Theory talks about Survival, but I talk about Safety & Security. If your actual physical survival is being threatened, you will be preoccupied with eliminating that threat, not worrying about how to better your relationship with yourself. It's the psychological aspect of the Survival need—Safety & Security—that you will be addressing. For this need, we will look at the relationship you have with money, your body, and your health. In order to feel Safe & Secure, it is important to feel satisfied in each of these areas.

I changed the name of the Power need to Significance because, due to the negative connotation of the word power, many people don't like to admit they have a high Power need. People with high Power needs are often perceived as control freaks, bullies, and obsessed with details. While these traits do describe some people with a high need for Power, many take a more responsible path—to make a difference, to have an impact, or to leave a legacy. Speaking about this need in terms of Significance is not only less stigmatizing, but also serves to describe people on both ends of the spectrum. To satisfy the

Significance need in your life, we will look at the relationship you have with control, your beliefs about your inherent value and worth, and your passion.

The need for Freedom obviously represents the need we all have to be unrestrained and independent. It also includes the need to be creative, authentic, and uninhibited. Freedom addresses the desires to be both psychologically and physically free. The aspects of our lives I associate with Freedom are the relationship you have with your environment, your relationship with self-created misery, and the relationship you have with your ability to be yourself.

I changed the name of the Fun need to Joy because when most people think of fun, they think of playing. The need for Joy is about much more than play; it's also your need to relax and learn things that are relevant and useful in your life. People like to be entertained, laugh, enjoy activities, learn new things, relax alone or with others, and find humor in things. The aspects of our lives I associate with Joy are your relationship with play, your relationship with relaxation, and your relationship with useful learning.

Finally, I call the need for Love & Belonging the need for Connection because it covers everything: your connection to your bowling team, your family, your friends, your job, your religious organization, your community, your music, and your pet. In this section, we will also address your relationship with your sexuality; your expectations; and your ideas, values and beliefs about the concept of love.

While writing this book, I learned that each person has an extremely personal perception of their basic needs and an equally unique Quality World. After reviewing chapters of this book, some of my colleagues remarked that an area I explored under the umbrella of Safety & Security, for them, fit better under Freedom. Others thought something under Freedom should go under Significance. Initially, this bothered me because I was struggling to find the "right" answer until I realized that we were all correct. In my own experience, certain aspects of my life are more applicable to one need; you may find those same aspects satisfy a different need. Because of this, don't get hung up on how I've categorized areas of your life and how they correspond to these basic needs.

I have come to know that my highest needs are Connection and Freedom, and because of that, I experience everything in my life through those lenses. We will talk more about this later when we discuss comfort zones.

For example, when my husband went through a bone marrow transplant, a Choice Theory friend of mine phoned me to check on how I was doing. I told him I was exhausted from being in the hospital all day, every day. He said, "Doesn't that meet your need for Power?" I said I didn't understand. He replied, "Well, you are being the best wife you can possibly be." After thinking a moment, I realized I had never felt more powerless in my life. My Power need was not being satisfied, but I was meeting my need for Connection. However, if my friend were in my shoes, he would have been satisfying his Power need.

It is rare that anything in your Quality World meets only one need. If something is central to your Quality World, it likely meets most, if not all, of your needs at the same time. While I may talk about your relationship with your expectations as part of the need for Connection, it's all right if that satisfies a different need for you than it does for me. The important thing is that you get to know each aspect of yourself as you create a loving, positive relationship with you.

There is no particular order in which to develop your relationship with yourself. Each aspect is important. You may discover you are already happy in some of the areas this book addresses. Celebrate those successes and turn your focus on the next aspect that interests you. You may want to start with what's easiest for you and work your way up to the most difficult, or you may want to tackle the hardest first and work your way backward. There are no rules. Work in whatever order seems natural for you. It will work best if you read the book cover to cover first and then come back to do the actual work of each chapter. Don't try to do it all at once. This journey is meant to be a marathon, not a sprint; take your time building this relationship with yourself. It will be the longest lasting, most important relationship you will ever have.

KNOWING YOURSELF—LOVING YOURSELF

"Finding your beauty isn't about looking exactly like everyone else. It's about accepting yourself—the parts you love and the parts you don't—and then working with all of it." – Scott Bames

According to Choice Theory, relationships start by meeting and getting to know someone. If the relationship feels good and meets at least one or more of the basic needs, that person will become someone you put in your Quality World. The Quality World is a mental area where you store all the things you've ever experienced, or hope to experience. The hopes and experiences stored in your Quality World feel really good to you and meet at least one or more of your basic human needs. The more need-satisfying a person is, the deeper the relationship will be embedded in your Quality World, and the more difficult it will be for you if it ends.

It's just a little bit different when developing a relationship with yourself. You already have a picture of yourself in your Quality World, whether it's your own ideal version of your Self or one you've created based on the expectations of others. You are constantly comparing your perception of yourself with the "perfect" ideal version in your Quality World; everyone finds themselves lacking when compared to perfection.

You might be surprised to know that even the most popular, successful, attractive, or athletic people have insecurities. Everybody can find themselves lacking at something until they discover that they are already "perfect" in every way that matters. We all are. It's important to focus your effort and energy on remembering you're perfectly imperfect.

Your life not only matters, but it is also important for humankind, whether you are here to influence one person or many. The Butterfly Effect tells us that changing one thing changes everything; you may never know the ripple effect of what you do, but please trust that everything you do has an impact. Whether you choose your path or follow a path someone has created for you, there will be an impact. There are no spare or defective parts. You have inherent value and worth.

You may not be athletic; that's not your gift. You may not be attractive; that's not your gift. You may not be popular or successful; those aren't your gifts. However, you are gifted in something, and you are capable of making a difference. After you accept your gift and use it to help yourself and others, many paths will become available to you that have the potential to impact people in a positive way. You were created "perfectly" for the fulfillment of that gift. I have discovered that finding purpose and being of service actually improves your relationship with your Self. That is how to meet your need for Significance.

Turn off the noise of everyone and everything else in your life, and listen to your inner voice whispering… or maybe it's screaming. Keep asking yourself, "What do I want to do regardless of what everyone thinks I should do?"

If you are unable to hear that inner voice, then you will need to turn down the volume of the external noise by spending more time with yourself—either experimenting with life or connecting with a Higher Power through meditation, nature, or prayer.

You need to create a Quality World picture of your Self as who you really are—the person you were created to be. As you begin to align your thoughts and behaviors to sync with that version of yourself, strengthening the relationship you have with the Self will follow naturally.

As you begin to like yourself more and more, you will solidify the best version of yourself in your Quality World. Then, when you compare the person you are with the person you want to be, there will be harmony. You will be measuring with the correct yardstick, instead of the stick someone else wants you to use.

You need to remember who you are; go back to that person you were before everyone else started telling you who you were and you believed them, or before you started to shape yourself into the false person you thought your boyfriend/girlfriend/mother/father wanted.

When you measure your behavior against the person you were created to be, then the rest won't matter. You will come to value the "real you," and you will know that you are safe; you are significant; you are free; you are joy; and you are love.

ARE YOU READY?

"When someone makes a decision, he is really diving into a strong current that will carry him to places he had never dreamed of when he first made the decision." – Paulo Coelho

Halfway through this book, I realized I forgot to implement the list of things I put together to help me take care of myself. Is that crazy? How does a person forget to take care of herself?

Sometimes you are so busy doing for others that you forget you need to take care of the vessel that performs those tasks. Other times, you forget about self-care because you don't prioritize it, and at the end of the day you say, "Oh shoot, I forgot about taking care of me today." The last reason for not doing self-care is that, perhaps, you don't think you're worth it.

Don't trick yourself into believing that doing self-care means rewarding yourself with an ice cream sundae or a new outfit. That is a trap, not true self-care. You can argue that, with their little nutritional value and amount of sugar, eating an ice cream sundae is more of an act of violence against yourself than self-care. Likewise, buying a new outfit may feel great, but it often has nothing to do with self-care and it may be counterproductive to your relationship with money.

When you are ready to begin taking care of yourself, you will read this book and take from it what you find relevant and useful. You will learn to let go of what isn't working in your life to make room for what does.

Some of you will read these chapters, and maybe you'll highlight some parts that particularly speak to you. But if you aren't ready to make the changes and let go of what isn't working in your life, then it won't matter how many people tell you to take care of yourself—you won't do it. No one can force you.

Before you go any further, I want you to ask yourself the question, "Do I really want to improve my life? Am I ready to prioritize myself over everyone else? Am I willing to do whatever it takes to let of go of what isn't working, even if those things are people I care about?" If the answer is no, put this book aside for a while. You aren't ready, and attempting to work through the book when you aren't ready won't help. In fact, it might do the opposite, because you might beat yourself up for failing.

People do not change until the pain of staying the same exceeds their fear of change. If you aren't in enough pain yet, then the things you are doing are still working in some small way. Have you ever stayed in a job or relationship much longer than you should? Looking back in hindsight, it's easy to see; however, when you are in that job or relationship, there is something about it that's working for you. Maybe it's matching your picture of being loyal, committed, and never giving up. Perhaps the little bit of appreciation or attention you were getting felt better than none at all.

The tendency is to stay in those painful situations until the pain reaches a level where your fear of the unknown is preferable to the pain of the current situation. How bad does it need to get before you are ready to love yourself more than you love anyone else?

Are you ready to get to know yourself better? Are you ready to put yourself first? Are you ready to really know your Self as safe, significant, free, joyful, and connected? If you are—even a little bit—then read on.

What Doesn't Work:

1. Prioritizing others when you are depleted yourself.
2. Ignoring coincidences that keep showing up in your life.
3. Focusing on your insecurities.
4. Allowing external noise to drown out your inner voice.
5. Judging yourself against a version of you created by others' expectations.

What Does:

1. Prioritizing your needs.
2. Giving attention to supposed "coincidences" in your life, particularly repeated ones.
3. Focusing on what you like most.
4. Paying attention to the relationship you forge with yourself.
4. Tuning into your inner voice.
5. Getting to know the "real" you.
6. Creating your own version of your "best" Self.

PERCEPTION

"If everyone could learn that what is right for me does not make it right for anyone else, the world would be a much happier place." – William Glasser

Much of what we believe to be true is based on perception, which is based on a myriad of things that are not absolute. Your perception is initially affected by your five senses; you cannot perceive anything outside of yourself until it interacts with one or more of your senses. Every moment, there are many things you are not privy to simply because you are not present. You have friends that live elsewhere, so you cannot know what they are doing without experiencing them in some way: a visit, phone call, text, or social media interaction. You cannot know for certain what other people think, even if they tell you, because you are not in their heads. Because you are one person limited to one place per moment, there is so much your senses are not exposed to.

It's not simply your senses, but their accuracy, that determine your perception. Perhaps your vision isn't the best; maybe you were born needing glasses or your 20/20 vision has begun to fade. Your taste buds and sense of smell are unique to you. You can like the taste of Brussels sprouts while others don't, and sniffing your favorite flower can cause your friend to sneeze. When it comes to music, there are people who are strictly fans of either heavy metal, country, hip hop, or jazz, and those who like them all. Why this is can be explained by the differences in how we perceive real world information taken in by our senses.

Focus also contributes to our difficulties in perception. For example, if you are absolutely focused on your task and someone tries to speak with you, you will miss the majority of what he or she is saying. Later, if you are asked to make a decision based on the previously provided information, it may not go well since you won't have all the information you need. For a wonderful example of missing the big picture due to focus, please watch the following two minute video: (*http://goo.gl/cchCr4*). This was an experiment with no consequences, but imagine if it was something important. If you didn't take the time to view the clip, see the note at the end of the page describing what you missed.[1]

The six blind men and the elephant is another example of faulty perception. In this parable, the blind men learn an elephant has come to their village, and never having experienced an elephant, they all go to place their hands on the animal. All six say different things. One says the elephant is like a rope, and the second says a solid pipe. The third feels a huge wall, and the fourth feels a big hand fan. The fifth man says the elephant is like a large pillar, and the last describes it as the branch of a tree. Of course, all were touching a different part of the elephant: in the same order, the tail, tusk, belly, ear, leg, and trunk. They could have argued about their different experiences forever, but a person who could see they were touching different parts of the elephant came along and enlightened them. But imagine if no such person came along. Each blind person experienced the elephant in different ways, and therefore, had their own unique ideas. Each went home and shared their idea of what an elephant is like, and their children shared with their children, who shared with their children, and so on. You can see how inaccurate information can come from faulty perceptions and

---

[1] *In the YouTube clip mentioned above, the narrator, Daniel Simons, asks viewers to count the number of times the basketball players in white uniforms pass the ball. After the players stop passing the ball, sixteen is revealed as the correct answer. Then Simons asks, "Did you spot the gorilla?" What gorilla? Replaying the clip without being focused on the players and their passes, you can easily see a person in a gorilla suit come onto the court from the right, stopping to beat its chest before continuing to exit the court on the left! You're probably amazed you didn't see it the first time; this is selective attention at work.*

experiences, and they sometimes can lead to generational beliefs and stereotypes based on inaccuracies.

In the summer of 2015, a picture of a dress was causing wars between friends and families on the Internet—it even made it to daily news shows. Due to the lighting, some people looked at the same picture and saw the dress how it really existed—blue and black stripes—while others saw white and gold. How can that be? The human experience is based on perceptions from our five senses, and these experiences are not always the same from one person to the next. It's a wonder we agree on anything at all.

When your senses experience new information, they send it to what Choice Theory calls the total knowledge filter. This filter in your brain contains the sum total of what you've experienced and information you have learned up to that point. For example, I know how to use a sewing machine, write a book, and play the piano. That information is in my total knowledge filter. You may know how to play soccer, cook gourmet meals, and create an Excel spreadsheet. No two people share exactly the same total knowledge filter, which partly explains how your perceptions can be different from others.

In 2016, the United States had one of the most contentious presidential elections I can remember in my lifetime—the race between Hillary Clinton and Donald Trump. What helped to make this election so contentious was that Democrats and Republicans were exposed to vastly different information from different news sources. "Fake news" emerged as a tool to divide and confuse, and the phrase "alternative facts" was born. When we perceive facts, we form opinions and beliefs—which are not facts—and people are allowed to disagree there. However, facts cannot be disputed because they are what they are. The phrase "alternative facts" wasn't about facts, but perceptions. My good friend Dr. Richard Doss says, "You can always find evidence to support anything you believe."

News sources have been catering to the perceptions of their advertisers, owners, and audiences; everyone likes to find information that agrees with their beliefs and have their perceptions solidified. If you tended toward liberal principles or favored Hillary Clinton, then you would tune in to CNN. If you wanted the more conservative view or favored Donald Trump, then you would tune in to FOX.

People like to be right, and that leads them to seek information that confirms what they already believe. Once you believe a certain thing, you generally do not go out into the world looking for contradicting information. When you do happen upon a contradiction, the tendency is to discount that information. You tend to look for supporting information and people with similar beliefs so you can feel justified. This is a very big world and no matter the belief, you can always find someone who will support it.

If you're rejecting the information from the previous paragraph, you may be finding it challenging to believe there can be different viewpoints based on information available.

Then comes the following questions: *Do I know enough? Have I exposed myself to enough information to be reasonably sure my perceptions are accurate?* When you are not *really* searching for truth, you will quickly answer this question in the affirmative. Thinking you know enough to support your beliefs is easier than attempting to see the bigger picture, as that requires searching for additional, and sometimes contradictory, information. If you are truly searching for truth, instead of looking in your usual places, seek information from those who think differently than you. Until you know the many sides of an issue, it is impossible to determine the truth.

Evan Spiegel, CEO of Snapchat, said, "Conforming happens so naturally that we can forget how powerful it is. But the thing that makes us human are those times we listen to the whispers of our soul and allow ourselves to be pulled in another direction." If you are striving to improve your relationship with your Self, you must look at perception as nothing absolute. Understand that values and beliefs are shaped by many factors; if something inside you is whispering a lack of surety, then seek more information.

The next filter that comes into play is your valuing filter.

All day long you experience information with your senses. All of the information you are exposed to, whether you have sought it out or unintentionally gathered it from others, is neutral information. It has no value until your valuing filter processes the information; this is where you decide whether it remains neutral or feels good or bad.

The information you have accumulated, the values of those you trust, and your own independent thought all affect your valuing filter. New information is judged depending on how you feel about it. If something matches how you want things to be, it feels great. If it goes against something you want, then it will feel bad. The vast majority of the information we process is neutral and doesn't feel particularly positive or negative.

Your values and beliefs are completely correct, but just for one person—you! You have created a value system based on your unique life: what you want, what you have experienced, and what you have learned from those you trust. Your values may work for you, but that doesn't mean they are going to work for anyone else. Your perception of your own values is skewed and distorted based on what you believe. You will likely surround yourself with people who share your value system; it feels comfortable to be surrounded by people who share your thoughts, beliefs, and values.

When you aren't confronted by people who think differently, you remain in your comfort zone with those who agree with you. If you are shaken by someone who thinks differently, you may be tempted to go back and ask those who agree with you to validate your way of thinking. This will help you reject the new, conflicting information so you can remain in your comfort zone.

The concept of a comfort zone is an interesting phenomenon. The very label of "comfort" implies a good thing. It brings to mind a favorite worn sweater, a cup of tea, or a great home cooked meal. However, remaining in a zone of comfort means you risk nothing and you learn nothing; comfort zones breed isolation and stagnation. Wanting to return to your comfort zone after risking, learning, and flourishing is acceptable; you are able to compare your comfort zone to the otherwise unknown world. Never leaving a place of comfort keeps you blind to other people, places, and values different from your own. Your comfort zone can be a place of ignorance, or, if you stray and return, an actual place of comfort. When you leave your original comfort zone to explore, it's unlikely you will return to your original. You have new information that might cause your old comfort zone to be not so comfortable anymore. It is more likely you will create a new and different comfort zone for yourself going forward. This will be further discussed in chapter seven.

If you want to learn, grow, and develop a stronger relationship with yourself, become curious about other's conflicting opinions. You will never have a shortage of people who think differently than you do, and it's easy to dismiss their opinions because they don't line up with yours. On the other hand, you can try to understand their way of thinking by seeing the world from where they stand. Being a person with your own unique knowledge filter will prevent you from gaining perfect clarity and understanding, but listening to those you initially disagree with expands your knowledge filter and helps you see a broader perspective. Your original perception may or may not change, but adding new information to your total knowledge filter will forever alter your future perceptions because you've learned something you didn't know before.

You can also give the power to shape your opinions, beliefs, and values to others. When you believe the approval of others is more important than being true to yourself, you lose yourself little by little as you adjust what you think to match those you have judged to be more important than you.

This process can happen imperceptibly. You can compromise yourself inch by inch, starting with something seemingly unimportant and, the next thing you know, you find you no longer recognize yourself—or worse, have no idea who you actually are.

Not to say you should be immoveable and unwilling to negotiate differences in your relationships, but get to know your

Self. During the Alone Stage of your relationships, discover what you like and what you don't; determine not only what your non-negotiables are, but also what you would be willing to be flexible with. The more you understand who you are, the less likely you will fall prey to the gradual erosion of your own identity.

Your choice to prioritize someone else's happiness over your own will lead to this erosion. Some of your perceptions and values are based on information you completely accepted without scrutiny as a child, usually from people you trusted. As you work toward choosing you now, you may want to closely examine your values and beliefs to determine which ones are serving you and which ones you might want to change.

EXTERNAL MESSAGES MADE INTERNAL

"Don't try to figure out what other people want to hear from you; figure out what you have to say. It's the one and only thing you have to offer."
– Barbara Kingsolver

Receiving information from others and adapting it as your own happens regularly. When you make a conscious decision to accept the information, it is helpful. On the other hand, what do you think happens when you subconsciously accept information as your own without having a choice.

EARLY CHILDHOOD MESSAGES

Some of the information in your total knowledge filter came from people you trusted as a child; this information may or may not be correct. It usually begins with the people that took care of you at a very young age, typically parents, but perhaps foster parents, grandparents, or family members. These people have their own faulty or accurate five senses, perspectives, beliefs, values, and perceptions. During their interactions with you, statements are made—some serious, others in jest—some intentional, some careless, and others completely unconscious. These statements vary widely: "You'll never amount to anything."

"You can be anything you set your mind to." "You get what you deserve in this world." "You don't get what you deserve, you get what you negotiate." "You're so smart." "You're so lazy." "You're adorable." "You're a chunky monkey."

When you begin to create a loving relationship with yourself, you will want to examine these early messages to determine the following:

1. Where did they come from?
2. Did I trust and respect the person who made them?
3. Did I believe that person had my best interest at heart?
4. Were they right?
5. How do I know? Can I be certain?
6. Where did they get their information?
7. Is it a truth for them that isn't necessarily true for me?
8. Does this information serve me and make me stronger, or does it belittle me and make me weaker?
9. What do I want to be true?
10. What steps do I need to take to make it so?

I once worked with a woman who had a challenging relationship with her mother. They loved each other but had difficulty understanding one another. They seemed to have very little in common; their values and beliefs were opposite on many issues.

One day she visited her mother and had an experience that illuminated early childhood messages she was previously unaware of. Her mother was talking about an outfit she bought that was quite dressy, wondering if she would get another opportunity to wear it. She was saying how she dislikes going places and being overdressed; she would rather be average or even underdressed so people won't believe she thinks she's better than anyone else. My client had no idea her mother felt that way, and she suddenly recognized those values and beliefs in herself—they weren't working for her.

She was a powerful business woman who often made public presentations. A year prior, she began wearing makeup and dressing in nice clothing. She had been dating a man who encouraged her to look her best, but she thought he was criticizing her and immediately became resistant to the idea. That conversation with her mother made her realize her inclination to downplay herself so others wouldn't think she thought she was better than they were.

I asked if she would be willing to go through the aforementioned ten-question process, and here are her answers:

Her belief: *I don't want to be the center of attention in a room. I want to blend in. I don't want anyone else to think I'm better than they are.*

1. Where did that come from? *My mother.*
2. Did I trust and respect the person? *Yes*
3. Did I believe that person had my best interest at heart? *Absolutely*
4. Were they right? *No*
5. How do I know? *The way I dress is an expression of my personality and how I feel about myself. It has nothing to do with anyone else around me.*
6. Where did my mother get her information? *I am not sure but it likely came from her mother, my grandmother.*
7. Is it a truth for her that isn't necessarily a truth for me? *Possibly. My mother likely believes others will not like her if she tries to "show off" or comes across as better off than others?*
8. Does this information serve me and make me stronger, or does it belittle me and make me weaker? *This information does not serve me or make me stronger. In fact, it is possible that others look to me to see how a strong, confident woman expresses herself. If I tone myself down to blend with everyone else, then I may not be of service to others who are looking for an example. However, what others think or don't think should not be the*

reason for what I choose to wear and how I present myself to the world.

9. What do I want to be true? *I want to express myself in line with how I feel and how I want to feel. When I am in professional settings, I want to wear makeup and dress in beautiful business clothes that uniquely express my personality and look good on my body. When I am with family and friends, I want to be comfortable enough to be my natural self, to not wear makeup, and to dress in comfortable clothing and shoes so I can be relaxed.*

10. What steps do I need to take to make it so? *There is nothing I need to do other than work through the steps I just went through. I now feel completely comfortable living my life in line with what I want to be true above. I am free from the beliefs and values of my mother and can move forward without that limitation in my head. In fact, what I want to be true has actually become true based on the choices I make.*

This is a bit of an innocuous example. What about the female client who feared if she made more money than her father did, he would be hurt and stop loving her? She also agreed to go through the ten-step process.

Her belief: *My father won't love me if I make more money than he does.*

1. Where did that come from? *My father.*
2. Did I trust and respect the person? *Without exception.*
3. Did I believe that person had my best interest at heart? *Yes*
4. Were they right? *This wasn't something my father believed, but a belief I developed based on some things I heard him say.*
5. How do I know? *My father spent his life trying to prove something to himself and others about his value and worth. He wanted to be the "best" and*

a success in everything he did and he generally was. However, he often lost interest in his current business venture and moved on. This created difficulty manifesting the monetary equivalent for all the work he expended. One time when I told him how much money I made for a job I was hired to do, he was shocked and appeared jealous. From that isolated conversation, I made a subconscious rule for myself: "I better not become more successful than Dad. It will hurt him and he might stop loving me."

6. Where did I get my information? *I totally made it up! It was fabricated out of thin air.*

7. Is it a truth for me that isn't necessarily a truth for him? *Absolutely! I know my father loves me unconditionally and applauds my financial success. It may cause a bit of nostalgia for his own missed opportunities, but in no way will it cause him to stop loving me. In fact, showing him my success will help him feel good about his life because, while he may not have had the success he was hoping for, he laid the groundwork for me to follow in his footsteps and exceed even beyond his own dreams.*

8. Does this information serve me and make me stronger or does it belittle me and make me weaker? *The story I was telling myself definitely held me back. Until I pulled this belief out of the darkness of my subconscious and into the light where I could see it for what it was, I was sabotaging my financial goals. I had stagnated at a plateau I couldn't exceed until I gained a new perspective. I didn't need my father's information or permission to tell myself a new story. I made up the first one that wasn't serving me; I was allowed to make up a new one that did!*

9. What do I want to be true? *The Universe is abundant. I will be fairly compensated for my*

service and I, in turn, will use that compensation to make my life and the lives of others better.

10. What steps do I need to take to make it so? *Every time I feel undeserving of financial abundance, I will remind myself that I am compensated based on the value I bring to the world. When I am fairly compensated, I am empowered to share that abundance with others—my family, the people I employ, the charities I support, and the government programs I help fund through the taxes I pay.*

What early childhood messages to you need to examine? It takes an honest view into your past, but begin to make an effort to uncover these messages and how they may have altered your perspective.

REPETITIVE ADULT MESSAGES

"Self-betrayal is allowing the fear voices to drown out the still, small voice that knows what to do and is always leading us home to ourselves and to truth and to love." – Glennon Doyle Melton

Repetitive messages in adulthood can be just as damaging as the ones you were defenseless against as a child. As adults, there may be times you believe you are dependent on others; when those people repeat messages to and about you, they can take their toll on your self-esteem. If you had a happy childhood but find yourself, as an adult, believing you have no value and no one could love you as you are, you are probably the victim of repetitive adult messages. Whenever this happens, you are ignoring your own voice and allowing others to control you.

ABUSE

You may find yourself in an abusive situation with no apparent avenue of escape; whether the prison is real or imaginary doesn't come into play. Abusive situations take many forms. You can marry into one; you can be a caregiver to your parents who berate you and say you're not good enough; you can be employed by someone with hierarchical and possibly financial power over you who belittles and harasses you. If you believe you can't escape, then you are right—you can't. Your abuser can leave the prison door open and you won't walk through because you have eventually come to imprison yourself.

What's insidious about these messages is that they are systematically designed to cause you to believe you are not good enough, you are less than, and no one else would ever want you. You come to believe you're trapped because no one would ever treat you any better.

Sometimes the abuse goes beyond verbal abuse to physical abuse. The abuser may have threatened to hurt or even kill you or someone you love if you leave; they hold something over you that keeps you in the abusive relationship. Sometimes you trap yourself in these situations. You may be religious, loyal, or loving enough to believe leaving is not something you could do.

Being in an abusive situation long enough, constantly exposed to repetitive messages designed to undermine your self-esteem, will often cause you to believe the terrible things being said about you. In this case, your perception is skewed by these untrue, hurtful repetitive messages which you have come to accept and believe.

CULTS

Cults are typically defined as unorthodox religious groups. If you have ever encountered a cult, you may notice similarities to abusive relationships. Cults often isolate their members to ensure there is no outside influence to contradict their teachings. They make it difficult for members to leave and often have norms that are not accepted by the greater society. The leader of a cult will use this societal disapproval to drive a wedge between its believers and outsiders, particularly loved ones.

Any outside, contradicting information is controlled so members will not be influenced by it. If you were to question the beliefs of a cult, they would likely threaten to ostracize you. The idea of social isolation from everything you know is often enough to keep you loyal to the cult.

Hearing the same information over and over again without any opposing information can create a situation where perception is seriously compromised.

BRAINWASHING

Brainwashing involves the restriction of information to control a person's perceptions. In the book, *Defiant*, author Alvin Townley writes about the strategies used by the North Vietnamese to control the perceptions of American prisoners of war. They broadcasted fabricated news reports about the United States ending the war and forgetting their POWs with the goal of breaking the prisoners and destroying their morale.

In 1969, Charles Manson was able to brainwash several of his followers into committing murder by constantly exposing them to his radical ideology. Repetitive messages can be extremely powerful, especially in the absence of outside information.

Patty Hearst was a young woman kidnapped by members of the Symbionese Liberation Army (SLA) in 1974. She was reportedly held blindfolded in a closet for several weeks with her life continuously being threatened. She was allowed to come out to eat and was subjected to the extreme political opinions of her captors. When she was given the opportunity to join them or die, she chose to join them and helped them commit crimes as a result.

In order to ascertain whether your perceptions are your own and not something instilled by someone else, you must ask the hard question, "Has my information been controlled? What happens when I attempt to research this information to learn other beliefs and opinions?"

If attempts to gain exposure to contradicting information are discouraged or forbidden, it's possible your beliefs and opinions are not your own. These are extreme examples, but versions of this can happen in normal, everyday life. If you receive limited information and your attempts to widen your perspective are blocked with threats, maybe of isolation or withdrawal of love and affection, then there is a good chance your opinions, values, and beliefs are not your own.

Take some time to get curious and expose yourself to people who think differently than you. Absorb new information while checking in with yourself to see if the new information suits you better than what you have been thinking to this point.

Influence of the Dominant Culture

Despite having written a book on diversity, I'm a member of the dominant culture, and I needed someone else to bring my attention to this important point. I was mortified that I hadn't, on my own, considered adding this to the "Early Childhood Messages" section of this book. I realized I didn't think about it because I don't have to think about it. So I made it my mission to speak with people I knew would be willing to share their experiences with me; of course, I found their experiences to be as diverse as they are. This section is a summary of information I received from people willing to talk with a heterosexual, white Christian about these important issues.

These differences in identity or cultural experiences can be classified as majority and minority cultures. There are places, like South Africa, where the majority culture is greater in number but is not dominant; despite being the minority, whites have historically held dominance there. For the sake of this book, I am using the term dominant culture in reference to the group who holds political and economic dominance.

Living in your country as a member of the non-dominant culture means you don't have the same rights, resources, opportunities, and advantages that are taken for granted by the dominant culture. Being a person of color, a member of the LGBTQ community, or a member of a minority religion can result in underrepresentation in politics and economic disadvantages. In many cases, the dominant culture will believe no such advantage exists. These advantages are known as privilege, and it can take many forms: male privilege, white privilege, Christian privilege, able-bodied privilege and heterosexual privilege, to name a few.

Consider the following questions:

- Have you ever been questioned, judged, or ostracized because of a part of yourself you can't change?
- Have you ever changed where you go because you felt unsafe in a majority culture situation?
- Have you ever been the only _____ in a room?
- Have you ever compromised your beliefs or convictions just to "fit in" with the majority culture?
- Have you ever attempted to deny aspects of yourself or your culture so you could assimilate to the dominate culture?
- Are there laws that discriminate against your culture?
- Have you had to educate your children about how to conduct themselves to protect them from violence due to their non-dominant cultural status?
- Have you ever been confronted by members of the dominant culture and feared for your life?

Unfortunately, many members of the non-dominant culture can answer yes to these questions and face this reality daily. This is pervasive, institutionalized discrimination against marginalized groups. People in the dominant culture may be able to remember a time when they could answer yes to one or two of those questions. Maybe you were bullied for being awkward, wearing glasses, having braces, or being overweight. Perhaps you had some toxic friends and changed yourself to appease them. Maybe you upset the wrong people and feared for your life. However, as part of the dominant culture, it's likely these situations were isolated or only occurred during a particular period of your life. These experiences are not a daily occurrence in multiple areas of your life. Being physically and emotionally safe in your own skin, as a member of your particular gender, sexual orientation, and religion, is a privilege inherited by the dominant culture.

It's similar to asking students sitting in a classroom to throw a ball of paper into a trash can at the front of the room. Those in the front of the class will have an advantage simply because of where they are seated. In the United States, white, able-bodied, heterosexual, Christian males are in the front, while the members of the non-dominant culture are in the back.

While members of the dominant culture may never have requested to sit in the front, they, nonetheless, have front row seats, priority, and privilege. "Sitting in the front" provides advantages in many areas over members of the non-dominant culture. It can even prevent those in the non-dominant culture from being rightfully recognized for their own accomplishments, or to have their struggles validated.

People in the back rows might be able to gain admission to the front, but at what cost? Will you need to work twice as hard for the same privilege? Will you need to acculturate, giving up a little of yourself and your personality to fit in? Will there be repercussions or accolades? How will your friends in the back be affected by your front row access?

Living without access to certain privileges can take its toll. It sends a message that members of the non-dominant culture are inferior to those in the dominant culture; people in the non-dominant culture may even agree, believing they have less value and worth. Some of the messages the non-dominant culture hears are incredibly discouraging: "You will never be accepted." "You are not good enough." "You will never have the same power as they do." "There's something wrong with you." "You aren't normal." "You will need to work twice as hard to gain the same privileges." "You won't be welcome there."

It was only five decades ago that African-Americans

gained the right to use the same bathrooms as Caucasians, eat at the same lunch counters, sit wherever they chose, and vote for elected officials. There was actually a law that stated southern blacks "counted" as 3/5 of a person. When the law classified blacks as less than a whole person, what message might that have instilled in people? Is it possible that it was carried on through generations?

Ever since the terrorist attack on September 11, 2001, the persecution of Muslims has greatly increased in the United States. They have been treated like criminals in their communities, watched more closely by the government, and even discriminated against by local establishments. Despite being the main victims of the extremist groups we group them with, we take our fear out on them.

It was only in 2015 when the Supreme Court legalized gay marriage in the United States. Prior to this decision, the partners of gay hospital patients were unable to attain information about their partner or spouse; they weren't classified as next of kin unless they went through multiple legal processes in advance. Many members of the LGBTQ do not feel comfortable or safe to place a photo of their loved one on their desk at work, let alone showing public displays of affection toward the one they love. So many, while going about their own business, have dealt with hearing they face eternal damnation, or that they are abnormal simply because they have a different sexual orientation. The lack of government interference, the confidence in displaying affection, and the absence of unprovoked discriminatory opinions are privileges the heterosexual community takes for granted.

In 2016, Native Americans fought in the Standing Rock Sioux Reservation for their right to land promised them in the 19th century. When you are a member of a non-dominant culture, the dominant culture has the ability to "renegotiate" terms of your agreements at any time. Though their protests were peaceful and full of prayer, they were reportedly met with a level of police brutality surprising for modern America: chemical warfare, water cannons in sub-freezing temperatures, and dog attacks. In 2017, President Trump signed an executive order that allowed the building of the pipeline they protested against. They didn't want it to ruin their only water source, which echoed the concern of Bismarck, ND, the city the pipeline was originally going to intersect. This city belonged to members of the dominant culture, so the pipeline was rerouted to affect non-dominant people.

Your loved ones may remind you of how special you are, and that you can accomplish anything you set your mind to. However, if there are hurtful, demeaning, marginalizing, and even violent messages being delivered to you by the dominant culture, you can start to believe those as well. These messages can become internalized and damage a person's self-esteem. These messages can also, however, serve as a catalyst for determination to prove the dominant culture wrong about their prejudiced, stereotypical views and beliefs.

In my book, *Secrets of Happy Couples*, I talk about having three options when you find yourself in situations or relationships you don't like—you can change it, you can accept it, or you can leave it. Depending on your perception, values, and opportunities, you may choose societally accepted options or you may choose options that can bring negative consequences.

Changing it usually involves working externally to fix the problem and typically has two possible outcomes—you can either make headway and feel good about your progress, or you can feel frustrated or dejected over your lack of any real progress. For the purposes of dominant/non-dominant culture, it can be done in a variety of ways:

1. Asking for what you want
2. Staging peaceful protests
3. Taking political action
4. Seeking equal privileges with the dominant culture through the courts and making laws
5. Confronting inequity whenever you see it
6. Using anger, violence, and/or hatred of the dominant culture

Accepting it involves accepting the reality that actually

exists. There *is* institutional and structural racism in the United States. Accepting it doesn't mean you have to agree with it, but it can offer some measure of peace. You are no longer fighting a system that is so much bigger than yourself, giving you room to see what *you*, personally, can do differently. This can feel more manageable because you are in complete control of you. Here are some positive and negative options that result from this method:

1. Putting in twice the effort to attain the privileges the dominant culture enjoys
2. Using positive affirmations about your inherent value and worth to counter the negative messages you receive from the dominant culture
3. Focusing on how proud you are of your accomplishments and the accomplishments of others in your non-dominant culture, despite having to operate within such a restrictive system
4. Giving up, withdrawing, and stopping attempts to improve your situation
5. Developing self-hatred and losing that important relationship you have with yourself

The final option is *leaving it*. Choosing to leave may not be possible for some non-dominant cultures. For example, African-Americans cannot change their skin color, but a Muslim or Orthodox Jew might decide to eliminate the use of their religious attire, and persons who are LGBT can hide their sexual orientation or gender identity. Here are some possible options should you decide to leave:

1. Acculturating to the dominant culture, looking and acting the way the dominant culture looks and acts on a full-time basis
2. Leaving your culture part-time to appease the dominant culture but staying true to your non-dominant culture when interacting with them
3. If possible, disguising yourself as a member of the dominant culture so you are afforded the same

privileges they have

4. Forming communities and organizations specifically for your particular culture that recognize you and your accomplishments

5. Abandoning your desire for a success identity and embracing an anti-social, sometimes criminal lifestyle. When you can't obtain the same privileges everyone else has, you may take them by force.

These choices are not mutually exclusive. Based on your own personality, you will choose to spend your energy on any of these options. There are no right or wrong answers here; every person's journey is unique. The goal is to create more love and affirmation for your Self by doing what works best for you in your situation.

Any of these options can bring mixed results. You may find yourself able to create the life you want and be happy about it. You may find yourself successful but feel guilty because of the people you've left behind. Combating the influences of the dominant culture can be exhausting as it requires your constant attention. The dominant culture may label you as angry, never happy, or bitter, and you end up feeling silenced and marginalized. Some members of the non-dominant culture will be happy for you; some will call you a "sell out." This rejection from your own culture may damage your self-esteem even more than the original messages you are attempting to combat. The possible experiences are endless.

To reach your overall goal of improving the relationship you have with your Self, you will want to recognize your unique gifts, talents, and abilities. Aspire to what brings you joy while helping other people. Only you can decide if that will happen from fighting the system, joining the system, or completely checking out.

Please know, there was not one moment when I felt comfortable writing this section. It was a difficult, but necessary, section to write. Being a woman is the only experience I have as a member of a non-dominant culture. Many people are members of multiple non-dominant cultures at once, being bombarded by the cumulative effects of multiple harmful messages. Whether you're part of the dominant or non-dominant culture, my hope is that this section brings opportunities for learning and understanding.

GOOD INTENTIONS

Sometimes there are people in your life who wish you well and want the best for you but, because of their own issues, find it best to discourage you from going after your dreams. Usually because of their own fears, they will encourage you to follow the safer path.

I have known people with spectacular talents in acting, performing, and writing who were told by their parents to do that as a hobby and find a job that would "pay the bills."

I knew a young girl who loved photography and was quite good at it. She was accepted into a prestigious photography school after her high school graduation. She was all set to attend when her parents talked her into going to a cosmetology school instead, convincing her the field of photography was too competitive to make an acceptable living.

There is no question these parents love, support, and encourage their children, but because of their own fears for their children's success, they can steer them away from their dreams.

When the recession hit hard, I had a new speaking and coaching business and the people who loved me told me I should probably look for a job. I'm so glad I didn't listen. It wasn't easy, but I was able to get through that challenging financial time by providing services people wanted and needed.

I recently spoke to an Indian-American who told me that when he was accepted into a medical school, there was no question he would become a doctor, even though he had no desire to be one. His family thought being a doctor was prestigious and would make a good living, something they wanted for their son. He did go to medical school but never finished. Now he owns and operates a successful spa, something he wanted to do.

Beware of well-intentioned people in your life who

cannot see your vision for happiness. When you have people you respect who have your best interests at heart, allow them to share their thoughts for your life. Hear them out and consider what they have to say. When looking at yourself, you sometimes have blind spots, but do not take everything well-meaning people say as absolute truth. They are not you, and they are not living your life. They do not have to live with the consequences of the decisions you make—you do. Check in with your inner sage. What do you want? Is what they are saying in line with what you believe is true? Is it based in fear and a shortage of confidence?

If their opinions help you move toward the life you want to live, then accept them as your own; however, if they don't, dismiss them. They are only someone else's thoughts about your life based on all their hopes and fears for you.

Sometimes it's those who care about us that can unwittingly become our worst enemy. Listen, consider, and decide the relevance of their advice for you and your life. Then make the decision you believe is best.

Relationship with Your Values and Priorities

"Things which matter most must never be at the mercy of things which matter least." – Johann Wolfgang von Goethe

How many times have you thought about what is really important to you? I grew up during a time of civil and women's rights, assertiveness classes, and values clarification. I have done many values clarification activities to determine which values are my highest. Want to try it?

OK, here goes… write down your seven most important values. These are my answers:

1. Family
2. Making a difference
3. Kindness
4. Integrity
5. Honesty

6. Freedom of Choice
7. Personal Responsibility

OK, now something happens and you have to give up two of them... *What?* OK, I'll let go of integrity and personal responsibility. Now you must live with only five values:

1. Family
2. Making a difference
3. Kindness
4. ~~Integrity~~
5. Honesty
6. Freedom of Choice
7. ~~Personal Responsibility~~

Now give up two more. *What? Are you kidding me?* OK, I'll give up making a difference and kindness. What will you scratch off your list? Now you're down to three.

1. Family
2. ~~Making a difference~~
3. ~~Kindness~~
4. ~~Integrity~~
5. Honesty
6. Freedom of Choice
7. ~~Personal Responsibility~~

Now, give up one more. *What? I can't choose.* You must choose. *OK, take free choice... you're killing me here!* Which two are left for you?

1. Family
2. ~~Making a difference~~
3. ~~Kindness~~
4. ~~Integrity~~
5. Honesty
6. ~~Freedom of Choice~~
7. Personal Responsibility

Yup, you guessed it. Take one more away. *All right, I'm numb now... just take honesty and be done with it.*

1. Family

2. ~~Making a difference~~
3. ~~Kindness~~
4. ~~Integrity~~
5. ~~Honesty~~
6. ~~Freedom of Choice~~
7. ~~Personal Responsibility~~

This means that Family is my number one value. What happened for you? What is your number one?

Now that you know your number one value, it's time to determine if your actions align with your values. Examine your values and determine if the time and energy you spend matches those values. Are you attending to the things that are most important to you, or are you engaging in activities others expect you to do? Do you know how to set personal boundaries, even if you lose something, in order to stay true to your values?

What I would ask myself is whether the amount of time and energy I expend each day is aligned with my value of family. For me, I can honestly say it is. What did you decide about your value alignment? When you are living a life aligned with your values, you improve the relationship you have with your Self. The opposite is also true—when your time and energy is predominately spent doing things that aren't important to you, then you will be out of integrity with your Self.

There are three things you can do to help with these situations. One is to ask yourself what your values mean to you. Just because my family is my number one value doesn't mean that I want to do everything for them. I also value freedom of choice... after all, it made it through three rounds of value clarification. It is very important to me that my children are independent and able to take care of themselves and their families. Making myself available every time they want me would not serve the highest good.

The next step is to analyze whether the time and energy you spend lines up with the hierarchy of your values. Do you spend more time in areas of your life that are not as important to you? Do you find your life is so busy with other things, you never get to what's important? Then, it would be wise to look at what you can let go of: maybe some of your commitments, change some of the things you do, or delegate to someone else.

The third step is to ask yourself if your values support or hurt you. Sometimes you may hold fast to a value that does you harm. For example, if you believe that all wealthy people are selfish, it may prevent you from connecting with a wealthy person who may be helpful or becoming wealthy yourself. It is a healthy exercise to check in with yourself on whether or not your values still serve you. When they don't, you can make the decision to hold fast to them anyway, or make adjustments by gaining new information and changing your perspective.

PERSPECTIVE

Perspective is crucial when you think about your priorities and how you spend your time. When you perceive your life as filled with "musts" and "have tos," it is difficult to feel free. You feel controlled by people and circumstances beyond your control and that is *never* good for you.

From a Choice Theory perspective, every single thing anyone ever does is because they *want* to. The problem is we sometimes lose sight of why we want to do things and we abdicate the responsibility to someone else, causing us to feel like the victim. I remember a co-worker I worked with a long time ago who hated her job and wished she could quit. She didn't so much mind the work, but she really disliked the manager. She wanted to quit on principle. The problem is, she believed she couldn't quit because her job was one-in-a-million. It gave her full-time health benefits for working only twenty hours a week. Her husband had a progressive, debilitative disease and her job was what paid his medical bills. She had to work, right?

It's all a matter of perspective. As long as she was telling herself she had to work at this "lousy" job, she was always going to experience that frustration eating her alive from the inside out! Unfortunately, the victim perspective is one many people choose. It *feels* right. *I don't want to work here but I have to, I must! It's not my fault. I'm stuck here; I'm trapped by my circumstances.* That pity party can get you a lot of things—attention, sympathy, justification, etc.

However, in order to be in good relationship with your emotions, you may want to change any victim perspective you are experiencing. Instead of looking at all the reasons you *don't* want to do the thing you are doing, ask yourself why you *want* to do it. In the case of my co-worker, she was working to provide healthcare for her sick husband. It was completely out of her love and respect for him. Imagine how her emotions would change if, instead of telling herself she had to work, she told herself, "I am working to take care of the man I love." It would change everything!

Next time you find yourself thinking you are doing something you don't want to do, stop and ask yourself, "If I truly don't want to do this, why am I choosing to?" If you can't find a valid reason, then don't do it. But if you can identify the reason, stop focusing on why you don't want to do it, and instead, focus on why you do. It will make the entire experience so much more enjoyable.

WHERE IS YOUR FOCUS?

"Come to know the power and authority of your graces with the same precision with which you have come to know your brokenness and pain."
– Caroline Myss

In the course of a day, there are a lot of things that happen. Your brain is wired to notice the negative—the things that aren't the way you want them to be. This is for survival purposes. Historically, it was most important to notice the saber-toothed tiger tracking you, the smoke in the air that signaled fire, and the signs of impending storms.

Today, there are few situations where your life is in imminent danger, and it serves you more to turn your mindful focus to what is going well in your life. This may not be "easy," but it can be developed with practice.

Those of you who follow me on Facebook will often see my posts ending with, "What's great about your day?" This is so I, myself, can focus on what's great about my day and so can others.

Naturally, challenging things happen. People have flat tires, get sick, lose jobs, and loved ones die. What could be positive about those things?

When my husband was dying, I read one of the most important books of my life thus far, *The Breakthrough Experience*, by John Demartini. In that book, he talked about the Periodic Table of Elements and how all the naturally occurring elements in our world have equal positive and negative value. There are always the same number of protons and electrons. From that fact, he extrapolated that our human experiences are the same with equally positive and negative aspects.

I read this book while my husband was dying with leukemia, and there was no way I could see anything positive about that! It didn't even seem right to ask the question, *What could be good or positive about this situation?* However, I was preparing for the possible eventuality and how I wanted to be resilient for my sons, so I broached that question with myself and came up with two answers. One was that we would have the opportunity to say goodbye, which is not something everyone gets. The second thing I thought of was that my husband, being a workaholic, would go to work at seven in the morning and not get home until somewhere between seven and nine at night. He worked Saturdays, and on Sundays he typically worked on his own cars—he was a mechanic. When he learned that the chemical benzene was suspected to be the causative agent in the type of leukemia he had, he stopped working long before he was too sick and unable to work.

Once he stopped working, my husband spent more time with my children in the four years he was sick than he would have had he lived to be one hundred. He coached their Little League and soccer teams; he took them hunting and taught them to work on cars. We took a family vacation to Disney World. We were granted the gift of time.

In no way did those two things by themselves balance out the overwhelming negativity of the loss of my husband and the father of my children. However, we later found several other positives. In all tragedy lies an equal balance of Gifts, Lessons, and Opportunities—I call this the GLO. In hindsight, it is fairly easy to find the GLO to balance out the pain. The real value comes from being able to find the GLO in the moment. Like any skill or habit, this requires practice, but it is possible for anyone.

Finding equal positives to balance the negative does not make the pain go away, but it will neutralize it so you are no longer paralyzed and can move forward from a healthy place.

This is different than being the eternal optimist; the opposite is also true. Whenever you are seeing a situation only as positive, circumstances will likely occur that humble you. There is nothing you can do to disturb the balance of the Universe. It isn't something you create; it's something you discover. It's always there, in every situation, without exception.

Life has balance. You get to choose the part you focus on, but that doesn't mean you deny the pain. It doesn't mean the bad stuff didn't happen; it simply means there is balance in all things. So however bad something is, there is equal positivity in it, no matter what. Decide to believe that, and focus on finding and highlighting the positive; then you will be strengthened and your resilience will expand. However, the choice is yours—you can choose to focus on the negative and more obvious, terrible parts of life's events. How good you become at recognizing the positive will be determined by how much you practice. Why not start now?

Think about the worst thing that ever happened to you. Try to come up with gifts, lessons, and opportunities that were the direct result of that terrible thing. You may not be able to equal things out on your first try, but the answers are there. You are only limited by your ability to find them.

One day while discussing this concept in a group therapy session, I asked the group to do the same exercise. There was a young heroin addict in the group, and when it was her turn to share, she admitted she couldn't find anything positive about finding her father dead, swinging from the end of a noose. After we talked for a while, she realized her father's suicide allowed both her and her sister to buy house with his life insurance money; it was the first time she had considered that benefit. That wasn't quite enough to equalize the loss of her father, but she was on her way to getting there. It's a process. Be patient with yourself while doing your best to maintain your positive focus.

What doesn't work:

1. Thinking your way is the only way.
2. Blindly accepting your values and beliefs as your own.
3. Allowing others, no matter how well-intentioned, to influence your inner knowing of what is best for your life.
4. Living out of sync with your values.
5. Telling yourself you "have to" do the things you do.
6. Believing bad things happen, especially to you.

What does:

1. Recognizing that perception is unique to each individual.
2. Examining your values and beliefs for authenticity.
3. Lining up your time and energy with the things that are most important to you.
4. Considering input from those you trust but trusting yourself most when it comes to knowing what is best for you.
5. Recognizing everything you do is because you want to do it and focusing on the reason for that.
6. Locating the gifts, lessons and opportunities in all experiences.

SAFETY & SECURITY

"At the end of the day, the goals are simple: safety and security." – Jodi Rell

*A*re you someone that prioritizes safety over most anything? Do you tend to avoid risky behavior? Do you worry a lot, not only about yourself but also about those close to you? Do you prioritize exercise, healthy eating, and other health-related behaviors? Do you like to plan for the long haul rather than embracing spontaneity? Are you someone that prefers saving to spending? Do you prefer to save up for a big purchase rather than buying on credit? Then you probably have a higher need for Safety & Security.

Even with a lower need for Safety & Security, it can seem like it's a priority when it isn't being met. If you find yourself in a threatening or dangerous situation, this need will be amplified. It will rise to the forefront when you are low on finances and living day-to-day. If you are facing a health crisis or in your older years, Safety & Security may feel more important to you than ever before.

The need hasn't grown or become stronger, you are just having greater difficulty meeting it now, so it captures your attention. Any time you feel anxious, worried, vulnerable, or scared, you are likely experiencing a depleted Safety & Security need. Sometimes you will recognize the source, and other times you will feel uneasy without being conscious of why.

It's also possible to have more Safety & Security than you actually need. You can be so consumed with this Safety & Security need that you never leave your home, making it difficult to satisfy other needs. You can spend so much time saving and planning for the future that you miss the spontaneity and opportunities of today. You can have an overprotective person in your life who attempts to control your every move so he or she can feel safer on your behalf.

When you have more Safety & Security than you require, you will start to feel other needs rising up. You'll crave more Freedom, Joy, Connection, and Significance. You will want to push against the manifestation of safety and security so your other needs can be met.

Consider the level of Safety & Security in your life. Based on how much you need to feel satisfied, do you have too much, not enough, or the perfect amount?

Ask yourself, "What can I do to increase the level of Safety & Security in my life?" Depending on your situation, you might consider taking a self-defense course, making some low-risk financial investments, eating healthier, or launching an exercise program.

You may have some rules that prevent you from feeling safe and secure. Perhaps you believe that if you don't worry, bad things will happen. You may use your fear of not having enough Safety & Security to get others to protect you. Your lack of security may prevent you from being generous with others, since you don't feel secure without banking every penny you have.

The power of perception comes into play with Safety & Security. Many times your Safety & Security concerns are over things that never happen. If you don't feel safe or secure, check whether your concerns are imminent. Is there a way to prepare for the worst but expect the best? Can you find a balance between preparation and freedom from worry?

Limiting beliefs can also affect your level of satisfaction with this need. You may tell yourself there will never be enough for you. You may focus on what is wrong in your life instead of what's right. Low self-esteem about your appearance can keep you from feeling satisfaction and security. Finally, you may have some limiting beliefs regarding your health. All of these beliefs will interfere with your level of satisfaction in Safety & Security.

Each need is a piece to this puzzle you're trying to

complete, so meeting the level of Safety & Security you need in your life is necessary to create a healthy relationship with your Self. Consider what you can improve to better satisfy your Safety & Security need. The relationship you have with your finances, your body, and your health are areas that I connected with Safety & Security. When these areas are in harmony with what I want in life, I feel safer and more secure.

When examining your relationship with this need, target your weakest areas. When you have a positive relationship with your finances, you are confident in your ability to get what you need to survive. You have your safety cushion, and you aren't consumed with worry over finances. Your relationship with your body is connected to Safety & Security because when you honestly appreciate what your body does for you, you can feel emotionally safe from ridicule about your insecurities or any shortcomings you perceive you have. Your relationship with your health is important because it is the one thing you have influence over that can prolong your life and improve your chances for survival.

These areas make sense for me, but you may have some other priorities. Whether or not they primarily meet your Safety & Security need, it is important to analyze how you feel, whether positively or negatively about yourself, in these areas.

RELATIONSHIP WITH MONEY

"Try paying the bills with love. The idea I am trying to espouse is that you can have both love and money, and be rich and generous." – T. Harv Eker

What is your relationship with money? Do you have as much as you want, or do you have limiting beliefs that keep money from flowing into your life? Do you see money as a way to help others or as a necessary evil? Do you think little money, little problems; big money, big problems? Are you always discounting the importance of money? Do you value money as the commodity that will support you in doing the things you find important?

As I searched for a quote for the beginning of this section, most of them professed the evil of money. The belief that money is evil and that wanting more is somehow wrong is the root of an unhappy relationship with money.

Money is not inherently good or evil, but simply an agreed upon currency exchange. In order to create a positive relationship with money, you must first appreciate the financial situation you are in.

This doesn't mean you necessarily want to stay in your current situation, but you need to have a genuine appreciation for the money you *do* have. If you find you're seriously lacking, then focus on what you are able to get with the limited money available to you. Some examples might be a roof over your head, heat in the winter, clothes to wear, and groceries in the refrigerator. Find a way to give thanks.

You can give thanks for supportive people in your life who might be willing to loan you money if you are in need. You can give thanks for programs designed to help you when you need them. Early in my business, I spent one winter collecting unemployment because I had no work scheduled at all. I was so grateful for unemployment, even though I knew I didn't want to stay there.

Once you are grateful for your current financial situation, then you can begin to examine the limiting beliefs you have around money, which many people have.

Complications come from the love and worship of money for money's sake. There are some people who prioritize accumulating wealth beyond anything they could possibly need it for, and for no reason other than to be able to say they have it. When people accumulate money to use as a tool to place energy, positivity, and abundance in the world, it can be an extremely positive thing.

According to Wikipedia, Oprah Winfrey has been ranked "the richest African-American, the greatest black philanthropist in American history, and is currently North America's first and only multi-billionaire black person." She was born into poverty to a single mother. How did she end up becoming a multi-billionaire? Rather than worshiping money, she clearly sees money as a tool and uses much of hers to help others.

If you have a higher Safety & Security need, it's important you have enough money in your bank account, safe investments, and cash on hand. Should the unexpected happen, you want to have insurance to cover you. This does not translate into the love of money but rather the need for security. Do not apologize for having this need.

People who aren't in high need of Safety & Security might criticize you for your cautious nature. Find all the ways you bring safety to those you love so you can feel good about your contributions to the world.

MY STORY

There was a time when my relationship with money created an obstacle to having a healthy relationship with my Self. In July of 2004, I was virtually debt-free. My house was paid for, I had no credit card debt, and all was well. I did have a car note for the first time in my life because in 2002, I purchased my very first new car, a red Toyota Celica with the action package. It was my dream car and the only thing on which I owed any money.

I always had a strong independent streak. In 2004, after working for other people my whole life, I decided to pack up most of my belongings in a U-Haul truck, with my car towing behind, and drive across the country to Chicago. There I would start my own business in a place where no one knew me. This created some challenges in the area of Safety & Security. Would I be safe in a big city? Would I be able to make enough money to pay my bills? Would I be so scared that I'd have to return to Pennsylvania as a failure?

So I was on my own in Chicago, where no one knew me, looking for independent work. It was scary.

I secured a line of credit on my house and because of my excellent credit rating, I had opened several 0% interest (for the first year) credit cards, at least three of them with $20,000 credit limits. Sounds like a *brilliant* financial plan, right? Do you see where this is going? At the time, I wonder why I couldn't.

I decided that for the first six months, I would basically read a lot, study, and figure out what I was doing. I had a $100,000 line of credit on my house, which I didn't touch. My plan was to use my 0% interest credit cards and, of course, pay them off before any interest started to accrue. That seemed like a solid plan to me.

For about six months, I read everything I could get my hands on about coaching and small business entrepreneurism. Being a licensed professional counselor certified in Reality Therapy and Choice Theory, the coaching part came fairly easy. It was the small business development that I knew nothing about. I was online a lot, trying to discover what the Internet was all about. I can't tell you how many email lists I signed up for to get all the "free" information I could find. I was too naïve to realize the "free" information was mostly a sales pitch to bait me into purchasing an upgrade. And, what the heck? I believed I needed what they were selling, so I spent a lot of money.

I had business coaches, went to workshops, and purchased multiple information products on the web. It was true I was learning a lot, but every time I learned something, it seemed to lead me to something else I needed to know and pay for, requiring a bigger financial investment in my business. That's how I always justified the spending—it was an "investment" in my business. What did I know about running a business? Nothing, so I learned, and the more I learned, I realized I needed to learn even more.

Finally, in January of 2005, I went to a business-building workshop with John Assaraf. You might remember him from *The Secret*. I got four main pieces of information from that workshop that were invaluable.

1. *If I wasn't making enough money, then I needed to double my prices.* Of course, I'd lose some clients so I'd want to have associates to whom I could refer my clients that were unable to pay my new rates.

2. *I couldn't do everything myself.* Actually I could, but

it would take me way too long to learn everything and become competent. I needed to find someone whose passion it was to do the things I didn't know how or didn't want to do. At that time, I was about to learn how to build a website. Back then, we were discouraged from using templates and were told we needed to build a website using HTML code. Because of this workshop, I was mercifully saved from learning all that. I hired an administrative assistant I couldn't afford, believing that hiring her would free me up to do more of what I am passionate about, things that would generate money for me. I started paying her $10/hour, and now I pay that same person $45/hour and she is worth every penny. Not once was there a time I was unable to pay her.

3. *If I really wanted to be considered an authority in my field, I needed to write a book.* I took a one-year online program to learn about self-publishing and, with a co-author, wrote my first book, *Leveraging Diversity at Work*. It was a great experience and netted me two amazing speaking engagements in 2007—one in Hawaii and one in Australia, among others.

4. *I was introduced to the power of the Law of Attraction.* John Assaraf talked a lot about visualizing and acting as if you already have the things you want. Doing this would mobilize the forces in the Universe to bring the resources and experiences into my life that I needed to accomplish my goals. He was extremely convincing; I believed in its power but had no clue how to make it work for me.

I continued further into debt. I don't have a high Safety & Security need, so I wasn't overly concerned about the spending. For months, I used my credit cards to pay my moving and living expenses. I used them to purchase a computer and pay for incidental business expenses such as stationery, Internet, business cards, a copy machine, a printer, a PO box, etc.—all the necessary business items to become a successful coach and consultant.

It was also in that year when I took the program to learn about self-publishing and with my co-author, Sylvester Baugh, published, *Leveraging Diversity at Work*. I never even thought about what I was spending because I knew everything I was doing was going to lead to my financial success, and I'd have all the money I needed to pay off the credit cards. No worries!

After taking that program for $5,000, I was convinced there would be more expense involved in writing my book if I didn't want it to look self-published. I had to hire the best cover designer, back cover copy writer, interior designer, content editor, and copy editor. I needed a team of people, the best I could find, because a weak link in any of those areas could mean the difference between being a bestselling author and having boxes of unsold books in my garage. Publishing Leveraging Diversity at Work amassed another $10,000 of debt.

During my first year, I learned about the power of affirmations, speaking my "truth" in advance to make my dreams come true. One of my affirmations during that time was, "I have zero balances on all my credit cards" and I got exactly what I affirmed! When my credit cards were going to begin charging me upwards of 20% annual interest rates, I hadn't yet become the successful business woman I thought I would be, and I couldn't pay off any of those credit cards. So, to avoid that serious credit card debt, I paid off the balances of those credit cards with my line of credit on my house in PA, resulting in zero balances on my credit cards—just what I had asked for. Instead of reducing my debt, I only succeeded in moving it from my credit cards to my line of credit. It didn't take long for me to max out my line of credit; when I did, my bank froze the line, making it impossible for me to borrow from it even after I had the balance paid down.

As for my successful business, I had done everything right. I had the business cards, the website, and the ability and intelligence to help people in need. I was good at what I did, proud of the business I built, but customers were not knocking down my doors. My first year in business, I made barely enough to meet my living expenses, let alone pay down the debt I had accumulated. I felt so disillusioned that my business wasn't thriving after a year of effort—actually, six months of research and then six months of serious effort. I may have had some unrealistic expectations that could be categorized as delusions of grandeur.

I was unwilling to abandon my dream of owning my own wildly successful business. As far as I could see, the only thing I could do was to further invest—in other words, go deeper into debt. I understood that this could either continue a serious downward spiral into bankruptcy, or it could accomplish the goal I was climbing toward—a successful coaching, speaking, and consulting business.

My first book did not sell well. I had spent more money than I ever thought possible on its production, so when it came to marketing and promotion, I had nothing left to invest. I met my goal in producing a self-published book that looked like it came from a publisher, but with my poor planning and lack of marketing, no one got to know about it. The books collected dust in my assistant's attic.

My second year in business, I managed to double my income. This sounds great, but any income I made was either being used to reinvest in my business or was eaten up by exorbitant interest rates. Despite being in serious financial trouble, I trudged on.

In 2008, I started thinking about writing a second book: *Secrets of Happy Couples: Loving Yourself, Your Partner and Your Life*. I wanted this book to help people in unhappy relationships, and I had no idea just how many people were in this category until I started doing the research. It took some time to write this book because I set a goal of interviewing one hundred happy couples. I defined happy couples as two people who had been together at least ten years and both separately stated they were happy in the relationship when the other person wasn't present. Many times, people claimed happiness while their partners confided the opposite. It was incredibly sad, but it confirmed I was on the right track—people needed to read what I was writing. However, it was going to require more money before I saw anything back from the investment.

Two years and many dollars later, I published *Secrets of Happy Couples*. I justified the cost by telling myself this book was going to be what would propel me out of debt, and it was truly a labor of love to help millions languishing in mediocre relationships. I had talked with one hundred happy couples, discovered the secrets of a happy relationship, and wanted to share these revelations with others.

I self-published again, though I learned from the mistakes I made with my first book. I needed to invest more in marketing, which I considered another investment in my business. It didn't matter that I was struggling to make my minimum payments while the interest kept adding up; my situation was desperate. By this time, my company was doing well, but the interest kept me drowning in debt and unable to get ahead.

No new credit card companies were interested in giving me more credit. I was a credit risk, but not because I didn't make payments, because I did; not once did I ever miss a payment. Whenever I worked hard to reduce a balance on a credit card, the company would reduce the card's limit so it looked as if I had maxed out my card again, when in fact, I had paid off a third of what I owed. I was trapped in this vicious cycle, feeling anxious and scared daily. I never knew whether I would have enough money to pay even the minimum balances.

How do you love yourself when you are in a deep, dark financial hole? I didn't have the answer to that at the time, so I wasn't very loving toward myself. Every week, I needed to set aside time to pay bills. With over twenty-five accounts that had balances on them, keeping my books and paying my bills was practically a full-time job. It was discouraging to watch how much I paid in interest. At the height of this problem, in one year I paid almost $24,000 just in interest! I am relieved to say that now the only interest I pay are on two mortgages.

You can probably imagine how discouraging and desperate it was. The things I would say to myself went something like this: "You're such a failure. You can't even pay your bills. You are going to die and leave nothing to your children. You are so stupid, how did you get yourself into this mess? What makes you think you will ever get out of this?" It's very difficult to love yourself when you are in such poor financial straits.

I knew I was in big trouble and needed some kind of help, so I searched for help in lots of financial books. Most of the books I read talked about paying yourself first, but when I could only manage the minimum credit card payments after paying my bills, I wasn't sure how I was going to do that. I couldn't pay one cent more than I already was; it was like treading water for months and even years at a time. How was I going to pay myself first and save 10% of my income? Impossible! Have you ever been there? It's where I lived.

I kept my heat at 65° in the winter and 78° in the summer. I told myself I couldn't afford anything that wasn't essential, so I was unable to buy clothes for myself or gifts for my sons and their families, including the seven grandchildren I now have. I was making a lot of money, but I owed a lot of money.

Many people in my situation would have filed for bankruptcy, as I was advised to do by three different financial planners. I considered it, but ultimately decided against it—I had my honor to protect. Along with my honor, I was scared to lose two investment properties I hoped to pass on to my sons. I had borrowed money with the promise I would pay it back, and I don't like going against my word. This is in no way an indictment against you if you have filed bankruptcy; you must make that decision based on what feels right to you. Bankruptcy can provide a sense of freedom and the ability to have a fresh start, but it just wasn't for me.

I kept my pride intact and my children's inheritance secure while I suffered through the dark years, hating myself for the financial mess I had made. I knew I needed help so I did what I know to do: I went to some financial workshops. While the information was great, it didn't fit my situation;

it was clearly not for people in as deep a debt as I had. There was no way I could save 10% of my income without accruing even more crushing interest and late fees.

It took a few months of mulling over the information before I came up with what I consider to be a brilliant plan. It got me out of serious credit card debt ($81,500 in five years!) without borrowing any money or ruining my credit score. If you find yourself in a serious financial situation and would like to learn about my plan, you can get the eBook for free here: *Get Out of Serious Debt without Harming Your Credit Score (https:// goo.gl/WMchNW).*

Hiring people to do the things I didn't know how, or didn't want to do, was a lesson from John Assaraf that rang true for me. I already had the assistant. I then began to delegate tasks that occupied my time: first it was social media, then scheduling, marketing, house cleaning and, most recently, bookkeeping and bill paying.

Examining the things in my life I didn't enjoy doing, and then hiring people who did enjoy those things, has freed me in a way that's difficult to explain. I now have more time to do the things I'm passionate about. I can say yes to more work that positively impacts people's lives, the work I love. I have time to take better care of myself in terms of getting more rest, exercise, and massages—I even have time to meditate and eat better. What can you delegate right now that would help someone else and increase your freedom?

I had to work on my mental and emotional beliefs around money and wealth. I had some biases holding me back; early childhood messages about money got in my way. One of my main beliefs was that wealthy people are self-centered and mean, which wasn't something I wanted to be, so my relationship with money was not a happy one. I often affirmed, "There is never enough money for what I need." I could remember my frugal mother frequently saying, "Money doesn't grow on trees, you know!"

I had to stop thinking of money as a necessary evil. Once I began thinking of it as a simple commodity exchange necessary for me to have a greater impact in my work, it began to flow into my life in a bigger way. I also feel good about using money to help enrich the lives of the people on my team. I have been able to transform my relationship with money from unhappy to grateful. How about you? Do you hold beliefs that keep money and wealth from flowing into your life?

Throughout this entire process, I learned discipline, acceptance, and eventually appreciation of my financial acumen. I've learned that negative and destructive beliefs about wealth not only prevent a healthy relationship with money, but they also get in the way of loving myself. I now have a very loving relationship with my finances and am proud of my accomplishments. I have built a successful business, repaid my debt and kept my credit rating intact. I no longer fear not knowing from where the next dollar will come.

The next area we will examine is the relationship you have with your body. Your body is the vessel that allows you to connect with others and complete your work—it is paramount to your sense of Safety & Security. When you have a positive relationship with your body, you will be safer and more secure.

RELATIONSHIP WITH YOUR BODY

"Beauty is about being comfortable in your own skin. It's about knowing and accepting who you are." – Ellen Degeneres

What do you see when you look in the mirror? When you understand how the brain works, you know it's hardwired for negativity. You search for and focus on what isn't right, what you don't like, and what's painful. Never is this truer than when you look in the mirror, either figuratively or literally. Sometimes it's the figurative mirror of who you are and what you do, and sometimes it's the literal mirror you use to measure your physical appearance. I once read the best diet in the world can be realized by eating naked in front of a mirror! Isn't that the truth?

I had a friend in high school who was constantly eating

bananas. When I asked her why, she said she heard they would help her gain weight. When she looked in the mirror, she judged herself too skinny!

What do you see when you look in the mirror? If you are like most, you see your flaws, which isn't helpful in creating a healthy relationship with your body.

You may not remember being two years-old, but most two year-olds I have seen are enamored with their reflection. Have you ever seen a young child delight in seeing themselves in the mirror? They often lean in to kiss themselves! When was the last time you felt that way when looking in the mirror? If you want to get back to that, then you need to start taking inventory of what you like about your reflection instead of what you don't.

For example, historically, I have not liked my thighs. They were an area of painful perception in my life since I was in college. They are large and it is the area where most of my cellulite resides... not a very happy place for me. When I used to look in the mirror, my thighs were the area my eyes were drawn to. Then my negative self-talk would kick in, "You're fat. How did you let yourself get to this point? Who would want to look at you? You have no self-control. What happened to your willpower, girl?" Then after giving myself a mental beating, I would think, "Oh screw it! I'm too far gone. I might as well enjoy this hot fudge sundae." It was a vicious cycle. I really hated this aspect of myself.

If you think about helping a friend lose weight, are these the comments you would make? Of course they aren't, so why do you do it with yourself? Criticizing yourself does not motivate—it demoralizes you.

So, with my body, I began with an affirmation, "I am thinner, stronger, and healthier every day. I easily and effortlessly release unwanted weight. I am love." I decided to say this every time I caught myself criticizing my body, so you can imagine I had many opportunities to say it each day. If you can't remember on your own, put an alert in your phone to remind you. At one point, my phone alerted me of this affirmation three times a day.

It is important to learn to love every aspect of yourself.

That doesn't mean there won't be areas you can improve upon, but it does mean you won't berate yourself whenever you look in the mirror or eat something you think you shouldn't.

When you are ashamed of your body, you will put more energy into hiding it than improving it. When you look in the mirror, hold gratitude in your heart for the body you have. Inventory the wonderful things your body allows you to do—walking, eating, jumping, running, breathing, digesting. Without the body you have, you wouldn't be able to live. Even if you think there is something wrong with your body, it is still your friend, it allows you to do so much that would be impossible without it.

As you age, you may notice things sagging and shifting in ways you don't like. You may find things you used to do effortlessly become difficult or even impossible. I must have been in my late forties when I decided to show my nieces how to do a cartwheel. I managed to execute it perfectly but almost broke my wrist in the process! Needless to say, I accepted the fact my cartwheeling days were over, but there are still many things I can do. When you are trying to build a healthy relationship with your Self, it is important to focus on what you can do rather than what you can't and on the here and now rather than the past or the future.

Once you are in harmony with your body, you will want to take a look at the relationship you have with your health. Having good health increases your sense of Safety & Security, particularly in terms of life expectancy.

RELATIONSHIP WITH YOUR HEALTH

"Keeping your body healthy is an expression of gratitude to the whole cosmos." – Thich Nhat Hanh

There are two types of health situations you may experience in your life—one is self-inflicted and within your control, and the other is something over which you have no control. For example, gaining so much weight you are experiencing joint pain and have contracted type II diabetes is self-inflicted, whereas learning you have lung cancer from living with a smoker is something you could not control. Bettering your relationship with health has to do with prioritizing, preserving, and protecting your health in the areas you can control and influence.

If you are reading this book and have excellent health, you may think this section does not apply to you, but it absolutely does. You may have excellent health but take that health for granted. You may suffer from the erroneous belief that since you are healthy now, you will always be so. This is not a given. Living in the moment does not mean you ignore the potential long-term consequences of your actions.

When you are creating a positive relationship with your Self, you realize your health is your most important possession. The healthier you are, the more energy you have to do the things that are important to you and, theoretically, the more time you will have to do them. Prioritizing your health means you will eat healthily, exercise regularly, and get enough rest.

This is the last area I am conquering on my self-love journey. It wouldn't matter that I created a happy and wonderful life for myself if I didn't have good health. I wouldn't be around or physically fit enough to enjoy it.

I remember hearing Suze Ormon, personal financial guru, once talk about how she could tell the size of a person's bank account by their weight. Her assertion was the less money a person had the more likely they would be overweight, which didn't make a lot of sense to me. I thought if a person didn't have much money, then they wouldn't have a lot to spend on food. I didn't consider what happens psychologically. When people restrict themselves from purchasing things that would enhance their lives, then food frequently becomes a convenient, and often subconscious, way of rewarding oneself. Also, people with less money buy food that is most affordable which unfortunately is rarely healthy. Another thing that happens is, when holding onto money in fear there will never be enough, your body can hold onto food as a result of that same scarcity mentality.

Whatever the reason, at fifty years old, I found myself

fifty pounds heavier than I should have been. This weight didn't appear overnight, but the accumulation definitely accelerated after I started my own business and got further into debt. I would "reward" myself with eating out, finishing with dessert for good measure; of course, I always cleaned my plate. As my weight increased, I was diagnosed with prehypertension. Twenty pounds later, I had sleep apnea and was diagnosed with high cholesterol. All of these conditions were most likely weight-related, something within my control.

In my defense, my lifestyle encouraged poor health habits. I traveled a lot, sleeping in hotels and eating in restaurants. It was difficult to maintain an exercise schedule. I didn't want to join a gym because I couldn't afford it; I wasn't even in town enough to make it worth the investment. Eating in restaurants makes it difficult to avoid hidden salt, fat, and sugar. All of these now sound like pitiful excuses.

While "rewarding" myself with food may sound like I was being loving toward myself, it was the exact opposite. How could rewarding yourself with something that's unhealthy, just because it tastes good, be considered a self-loving action? Jack Canfield once said, "Nothing tastes as good as thin feels." I heard it, acknowledged it, and continued to "reward" myself with things that tasted good but were not good for me.

I didn't love my body enough to move it on a regular basis. I do not like to exercise for exercise's sake, but I like to do physical things with other people for a purpose. For example, I like to go hiking or climbing with people. I like walking with friends whom I enjoy. I love to swim but hated how I looked in a bathing suit, so swimming was out of the question!

The self-loathing I developed over my weight was serious. I stopped looking at myself in the mirror and bought clothes that covered up my body, but who was I kidding? No material could cover up my size. If thoughts become reality, then I was creating more weight for myself. I constantly thought about my weight. I had an everyday reminder of the damage I was doing to myself in the form of the Atenolol pill I took to reduce my blood pressure, but it wasn't yet enough for me to sustain any real change.

I had a bit of a wakeup call in the form of an accident. In November of 2014, I was working in Scottsdale, AZ and scheduled an extra day to enjoy the area. My work was done and I decided to take my first hot air balloon ride. Because I had been working, I was alone in Arizona and went on this adventure by myself; this was a monumental feat for me because I normally don't do recreational things by myself. If given the choice between doing something fun alone or staying home, I would opt to stay home, believing things wouldn't be any fun if I didn't have a shared experience. I was attempting to break that habit when I booked this excursion.

It was everything I thought it would be. It was beautiful up in the sky, looking down on the rugged terrain. Our pilot, Walt, was quite knowledgeable about the local history, flora and fauna and kept us all entertained. At one point, Walt prepared us for a possible crash landing. He shared how we were to stand upon landing so the basket wouldn't flop forward. It was a little like the safety briefing flight attendants give when taking off in an airplane. You only half-listen, believing you are never going to need that information.

As we were preparing to land, I later learned, there was some unforecast wind. On our descent, everything seemed to be going well. What did I know? It was my first experience! The pilot seemed a bit on edge when he told us to "assume the position." We all braced ourselves with one shoulder against the forward part of the basket, one leg bent and the other out rigid behind us for stability.

The next thing I knew, Walt told us he was going to "bounce us off some creosote bushes." He said, "Around here, we call them balloon brakes!" He made it sound so normal, I wasn't at all worried. Then I saw we were being propelled by the wind, horizontally parallel to the ground, straight toward a mountain! I later learned from the accident report that the pilot had attempted to take us back up in the air to go over that mountain but a valve stuck, making it impossible to rise again, so we continued to bounce off whatever creosote bushes there were. At one point, there was a huge impact underneath my feet and I was pretty sure I broke my right ankle. About thirty seconds later, there was a second impact right under where I standing and I knew I broke my left ankle. Later, I learned we had hit an ironwood tree, and they don't call them ironwood for no reason! The pilot told us to "hunker down" as the pieces of creosote bushes flew in the air, coming up and over the basket.

I don't actually remember landing, but I was surprised to find us all on our stomachs rather than standing upright. The pilot jumped out of the basket and ran down the row, asking everyone if they were all right. I was the last person in the basket and when he asked me, I calmly said, "I think I broke my ankles." Walt admitted he didn't think my ankles could be broken because I wasn't screaming and I was too calm. I don't know why, perhaps I was in shock, but I wasn't experiencing serious pain.

Everyone else got out of the basket and I was asked to stay where I was. We landed in the middle of the dessert, a distance from the nearest road, and our pickup vehicle had yet to arrive. After laying there for a while, I wanted to sit up, which required moving my legs and allowing them to hang over the basket. When I managed to get in that position, my leg was pointing forward and my left foot was pointing to the left at an unnatural 45° angle. There happened to be two EMTs in our party, and one of them immediately said, "Yup, you broke your ankle, all right!"

I remained very calm, unusually so. One of my first thoughts was, *Well Kim, now you have the opportunity to practice what you preach.*

Choice Theory psychology tells me I have little control over the things that happen in my life, but I have 100% control over how I respond. Here I was with one badly broken ankle, maybe two broken ankles, and I had a choice. I didn't have a choice about walking—I wasn't able to do that. My choice was to feel sorry for myself or make the most of the situation. I opted for the latter and never looked back.

I was carried to a van that became an emergency

transport, bringing the injured over the rough desert terrain to a highway that eventually led us to the emergency room. I worked hard to appear nonchalant as we bounced over the ruts, stones, and other bumps along the way. At one point my left foot swung freely from side to side, and I remember thinking that it was detached from the rest of my body! Of course that wasn't the case, but that is what my shocked mind told myself. The others in the van remarked about how well I was handling everything. I know I didn't want to cause any of them any undue stress, nor did I want to give in to the worry and fear that could have consumed me.

During rehabilitation, I felt incredibly grateful for the legs I usually criticized. I felt fortunate to have two legs, even while broken, knowing they would work again to get me from one place to another. I never wanted to take my health for granted again.

However, without putting in the effort necessary to create new habits, you are destined to return to past behaviors. Once I was able to walk again and resume my work schedule, I quickly forgot to be grateful for my legs and went back to the criticism.

My relationship with my body and my health are not what I want them to be, but I'm making slow and steady progress, working on forming new habits. Weight loss may take care of all three issues—prehypertension, sleep apnea, and high cholesterol. I do something to exercise my body every day and am making better food choices when I eat out, like leaving with leftovers rather than cleaning my plate.

My Safety & Security need is not very high; my Freedom need is. In order for me to be happy, I require a lot of freedom, which I often experienced by eating things that taste great. At some point, it will become most important for my relationship with my Self to either make choices that improve my health, or accept that I value my freedom more than my health.

The ultimate goal is to create a sense of peace with who I am and what is most important to me. Instead of choosing to either improve my health or maintain my freedom, what if

I could improve my health while creating more freedom? In my work, I've always advocated for "both/and" solutions rather than "either/or" decisions. So I decided to, again, practice what I preach. I've been making healthier choices through diet and exercise while creating opportunities for freedom in other areas of my life. Secondly, I am working on shifting my perception on diet and exercise from restrictive to freeing. Improved health will give me a greater ability to be active with my grandchildren, freedom from joint aches and pains that come from being overweight, and, overall, it will likely give me more time in my life.

Taking care of my health is my responsibility. It isn't up to anyone else, and I don't want to take the easy artificial route of taking pills when there are natural things I can do.

I didn't want to master every aspect of this book before writing it; I hope that sharing my struggles makes it real and more relatable. I am not perfect. In fact, I wrote this book to aid me in creating a good relationship with myself. Some areas are easier for me than others, as they will be for you. Don't allow one of the hard parts to derail you from the overall goal of loving your Self. It is a step-by-step process: ridding yourself of what doesn't work while making room for what does, one thing at a time.

When you are working to prioritize your health, there are three steps: prioritizing, preserving, and protecting.

Prioritizing

Eating well means different things for different people. For some, it can mean a whole, organic, or Paleo diet. Others will want to cut out simple carbohydrates. Some will use portion control, and others will eat whatever they want while balancing it with physical activity. Loving your Self means finding foods that allow you to be at your best, maintaining a healthy weight, and creating the mindset that doing so brings about more freedom than just eating whatever you want. When you prioritize your health, you will stop taking it for granted while recognizing the importance of it and the power you have for maintaining it.

PRESERVING

After prioritizing your health, the next step is to preserve it. Exercise is very important in preserving your health. Your body is a miraculous machine that will continue to do miraculous things as long as you maintain using it. If you are like me with a job that tends toward inactivity, set aside time each day to move your body in ways you enjoy. If you tell yourself exercise is something you *have* to do but hate doing it, you will be much less likely to engage in it. There are three types of exercise that are all important to your overall health; incorporate cardio, strength-building and flexibility into your routine.

It is important to find the *why* of exercise that resonates with you. You exercise and eat healthy because you care about yourself. You want to extend your physical abilities and the time you have to enjoy the things you love in life. My reason is that I want to be around to enjoy my grandchildren while also being physically active in the process. What is your reason for preserving your health?

PROTECTING

Don't let anyone or anything get in the way of you doing what you want to do about your health—protect it. Without a positive, loving relationship with your Self, you will often allow other things to interfere with your best laid plans. You may prioritize your health without protecting your time and activities around that, allowing other people and things to interfere. It is important to remember that establishing and maintaining positive health practices is the very thing that will allow you to be able to serve others. Protect that time.

Here are some things to help you on this journey:

1. Remember the goal is to be healthy and comfortable in your own skin.
2. In the midst of a craving, remember that you could eat whatever you want but, right now, you don't want to. This will keep you from feeling deprived

all the time. If the craving persists, go ahead and indulge marginally with a couple of bites instead of an entire serving.

3. Schedule your workout time the night before, especially when you don't always have a predictable schedule and working out first thing in the morning isn't always possible. Look at your schedule for the day and decide when you will exercise, and calendar it.

4. When you hear the little voice in your head saying, "You can skip today; it's no big deal," remember your reason for being healthy. Remind yourself of your reason often.

5. When you think you are hungry, drink a glass of water first. Sometimes perceived hunger is actually thirst in disguise.

6. When feeling hungry, use mindfulness to key into your body signals and ask yourself, *Am I really hungry?* Sometimes, you aren't actually hungry, but you are bored, stressed, or feeling some other emotional response that has been paired with eating. If you determine you actually are hungry, then eat, but eat slowly so you don't overeat.

7. Every hour, whenever feasible, get up and walk at least 250 steps. I have a Fitbit that reminds me to do so and appreciate the reminder to move. I was capable of sitting for sixteen hours a day working, getting up only to eat, drink, and use the bathroom. That is incredibly unhealthy!

The idea is to find things that will help you stay on track and minimize that voice in your head that lies about how unimportant exercise is and convinces you to reward yourself with an unhealthy snack.

There is so much more involved in your relationship with your health and body. If you are looking for more information on this subject, such as the benefits people can get from overeating and not exercising, you might be interested in my eBook, *Weight Loss from the InsideOut.* You can learn more about it here: (*http://goo.gl/yxE2Lt.*)

It's important to move your body so you don't lose the ability to, and eating healthy is a great way to love your Self. Don't be fooled by short-lived indulgence; think of sugary snacks as poison instead of a reward. If you are truly loving your Self, why would you assault yourself in that way? Be kind and loving by providing healthy fuel and movement for your body.

If you want more Safety & Security in your life, then be more safe and secure. Prepare for the things that concern you so you can be more present. Invest your savings so you will have it when you need it, and avoid large debt. Do what's reasonable and within your power to maintain and improve your health. Rid yourself of the limiting beliefs you have surrounding your finances, body, and health.

When you reach the needed level of Safety & Security in your life, you will be able to focus on your other needs: Significance, Freedom, Joy and Connection.

What doesn't work:

1. Spending money you don't have.
2. Paying only minimum balances on high interest credit cards.
3. Saving money without having any fun.
4. Spending money without any savings.
5. Attempting to do everything yourself.
6. Criticizing those things about your body you do not like.
7. Focusing on things you can't do.
8. Inactivity.
9. Rewarding yourself with food.
10. Eating for emotional reasons.
11. Eating when not hungry.

What does:

1. Creating and following a debt reduction plan.
2. Paying cash for things you buy or paying off the full balance of credit cards each month.
3. Creating a healthy balance for you between spending and saving.
4. Eating healthy food.
5. Delegating those things you don't want to do to others who love doing them.
6. Appreciating every aspect of your body, if not its appearance, at least its function.
7. Focusing on and appreciating the things you can do.
8. Moving your body purposely daily.
9. Eating healthy food.
10. Drinking lots of water.
11. Eating only when hungry and stop eating when the hunger is sated.

SIGNIFICANCE

"You get your confidence and intuition back by trusting yourself, by being militantly on your own side." – Anne Lamott

*A*re you someone who prioritizes respect over most everything else? Do you tend to get upset when you don't get the recognition you deserve? Do you feel you must make a difference in this world during your lifetime? Do you like to be right and have the last word? Is it imperative you leave a legacy after you are gone? Is winning important to you? Are you focused on always improving your skills? Do you like to be in control of what is happening around you? Everyone is born with a need for Significance, but if you answered yes to most of those questions, it's likely your need for Significance is higher than average.

There are three ways to improve your level of Significance. Firstly, you can try to control everything around you, including other people in your life. Secondly, you can cooperatively work together with others to accomplish a common goal. Thirdly, you can develop your gifts, talents, and abilities to serve others. The first way is not responsible because it prevents those you are controlling from meeting their needs. The second way is legitimate, but it requires something you do not always have control over—the cooperation of others. For the purposes of improving the relationship you have with your Self, we will focus on the third way to increase Significance.

When your levels of Significance are low, you may find yourself feeling small, as if nothing you do has any impact. You may think no one even notices you. Times like these can find you feeling jealous of others' successes. You may also be feeling disrespected or under-appreciated for the things you do. Low levels of Significance can have you spinning out-of-control, holding on for dear life. Assess your current level of Significance. Is it proportionate to your wants and needs, or could you use more or less Significance in your life?

Even with a lower need for Significance, it will be a priority when it isn't being met. You might feel the absence of Significance when other people are getting what you thought you deserved. When life presents you with situations you cannot control, you can lose your sense of Significance. If others take credit for your work or fail to provide you recognition, you may feel the importance of Significance. When no one is listening and you're wanting to be understood, your level of Significance could reach a low point. It's not that the need has grown stronger, you are just having a more difficult time meeting it.

It's also possible to have more Significance than you need. Maybe that promotion at work gave you more responsibilities than you want to manage. Perhaps being an expert in your field causes people to constantly want your help and attention, making it difficult for you to have any privacy or free time. It's possible people have elevated you to a level you are uncomfortable with, not wanting the extra attention and feeling like you are no better than anyone else. This can feel just as frustrating as not having enough Significance.

If you find you need more Significance in your life, you might consider developing new skills or improving an old competence you possess. You may volunteer somewhere to make a difference in the lives of people who are not as fortunate as you. Needing more Significance requires you to *be* more significant. What would that look like for you?

A low level of Significance cannot be fixed with more Connection, Safety, Freedom or Joy—Significance is what you need. I knew a woman who tried to get promoted by having sex with the boss. While it may temporarily increase her perception of Significance, it isn't authentic so it won't satisfy for long. If you need Significance, remember you are important and you *do* matter.

You may have some rules regarding Significance. Many women from my generation were taught to be careful of becoming more successful than their husbands. Making more money or having more prestige could make your husband feel insecure. Your friends and family may exhibit jealousy when you are all that you can be. These often subconscious rules may cause you to dim your own light so those around you won't feel inadequate. I'd like you to challenge your perception about this.

Telling yourself people need you to be less to feel better about themselves is a matter of perception. What if the opposite were true? What if they need you to guide them toward claiming their own significance? When you step into your own significance, there may be people in your life who will disconnect from you. It's okay, because these people aren't the ones who will help you reach your aspirations. If you have become so great that people need to exit your life, it is not *your* shortcoming. They were there when you needed them, but that time has passed. You can continue loving them from a distance, wish them well, and move on. They may reconsider and come back, but don't dwell on the possibility. Continue forward on your path.

There are many powerful limiting beliefs around the need for Significance. You may believe you are not good enough, lacking the intelligence or the talent to reach your goals. You may believe something or someone from your past is holding you back. You may be afraid to leave your comfort zone and strive for more; failure may scare you, but so can the effects that success can have on your life. You may believe becoming more of your Self is more than you deserve or have a right to ask for. You may believe people who tell you they know best, causing you to mistrust your Self. All of these beliefs, whether conscious or subconscious, will distract you and hold you back from becoming all that you were meant to be. Don't fall prey to these limits; let your Self soar.

When I looked at the Significance need, I thought of the relationship I have with control, particularly with whether I work to control myself or others; this has a huge impact on how powerful we feel at the end of the day. Working hard to control others may temporarily satisfy you, but it doesn't address that inherent drive that really matters. That is connected to helping others, not controlling or destroying them.

Based on things you may have learned that were untrue, you might believe you have more or less value than others. It is important to understand that each human has the same inherent value and worth. Your perception and the perception of others may cause you to think some people are more valuable than others, but this is a lie.

When you live in alignment with your values, sharing your gifts, talents, and abilities to benefit others, it may appear to yourself and others that your life is more valuable. However, this just means you feel good and are realizing the impact you're making. Your life matters.

Meeting your need for Significance is an important part of creating a healthy relationship with yourself. Let go of what isn't working for you in order to create room for the things that will. This often requires a leap of faith. What are the ways you can create Significance in your life? Let's take a look at these areas: your relationship with control, your inherent value and worth, and your passion. Creating a positive relationship with your Self in the area of Significance is essential in discovering who you really are.

RELATIONSHIP WITH CONTROL

"Accept – then act. Whatever the present moment contains, accept it as if you had chosen it." – Eckhart Tolle

Choice Theory proposes that you choose what you do because of what is happening inside you—mainly what you most want in that moment based on your five basic needs. You do not respond based on external events and other people. Anything external simply provides information that will factor into what you want most in that moment.

For example, I am sitting at my computer, writing

what will eventually become the book, *Choosing Me Now*. It is important to me, and it's what I want most in this moment. However, if someone walks in, puts a gun to my head, and tells me to give him my purse, I will likely choose to get up, get my purse, and hand it over to him. My book is still important to me, but staying alive has suddenly taken precedence over completing this book. The man with the gun didn't *make* me do as he asked. He merely provided me with information that allowed me to reorder my priorities!

This may seem like a small distinction to you but, for the sake of your happiness, it is a crucial distinction. When you go through life believing that you're controlled by outside events, circumstances, and other people, it makes for an unhappy life.

You want to be the master of your own universe, the determiner of your own destiny; therefore, believing you are controlled by anything outside yourself is counter to what you want, resulting in your unhappiness and frustration.

This realization comes with a flip-side that is both freeing and frustrating. After realizing you are acting based on what is most important to you at the time, you must also accept that others are as well. This translates into the understanding that you cannot control others, no matter how much you want to.

When I ask audiences, "Whose behavior can you control?" they always know the answer… *their own!* However, when I follow up with the question, "Whose behavior do you try to control all day long," they predictably answer, "Everyone else's!" Is this also true for you? On the surface, it seems easier to change others instead of changing yourself. This is a fallacy, however, since your power lies in the ability to control yourself.

Your personal relationship with control is one of the most important aspects of how you relate to your Self and others. Understanding that you, and you alone, control yourself—no one can make you do anything you do not *want* to do—is paramount in developing a healthy relationship with your Self. So too is the converse; it is neither your right, nor your responsibility, to attempt to control anyone else in your life. All you can do is provide others with information so they can make informed decisions based on what is most important to them.

It is one thing to understand this and quite another to put it into action. When you accept and begin living these concepts, the following benefits will emerge:

1. You will take responsibility for the decisions you make and the actions you take.
2. You will allow others the right to make the decisions that are best for them without interference, without using coercion or your emotions to attempt to anger, guilt or depress anyone into doing things your way.
3. You will stop talking about things you *have* to do while realizing every single thing you do is because you actually *want* to.
4. You will stop wasting time feeling victimized by circumstances beyond your control. Instead, you will start figuring out the next thing you want to do in response to what has happened already.
5. You will stop regretting things from your past, as well as being anxious about your future, while appreciating the present moment.
6. You will focus your energy and resources on what you can do in this moment to maximize what you want most.

Maybe you are in a relationship with someone, and you want to have dinner at your parents' home. Your partner doesn't want to go and says so. Instead of sulking to guilt him into going, you will make the decision to go alone, invite a friend, or stay home.

With children, you may want them to do something they don't want to do. I know a woman whose son loves baseball. He wants to be a professional player and is hopeful he'll get a college scholarship. The mother wants him to play golf instead because she believes the likelihood of a golf scholarship is higher than a baseball one. She can provide that information to her son, but she must allow him to make that decision himself.

RESPONSIBILITY

"While you can't keep your heart from being broken, you can stop breaking your own heart . . . once you realize the difference between what you can control and what you can't, and that it's far, far more fun to lavish that attention on your own self-worth." – Leigh Newman

Once you understand that no one else can *make* you do anything, you will no longer blame others for your choices. Of course, you *can* still choose to blame others, but this untrue excuse will cease to be as satisfying. Wherever you are in life is the sum total of your genetics, your experiences, and your choices. Where you go from there is a direct result of the choices you make; remember, choosing to do nothing is also a choice.

Taking responsibility for your place in life has no element of blame to it. It doesn't mean you berate yourself, but you accept your position is a result of your choices, the things you did or failed to do. It is merely a fact—no judgment involved. Only after accepting this, without blame or judgment, can you decide where you want to be and begin taking steps to get there. There is no sense in accepting responsibility if you are only going to criticize yourself for your choices.

Criticism creates suffering, not improvement. People can inform you about things you don't know or can't see that help you improve. They aren't necessarily criticizing; they are sharing new information you may accept or reject. When someone criticizes you, the criticizer assumes he or she knows better than you and expects you to change whether you want to or not. It is never helpful, unless it is used as inspiration to prove the criticizer wrong. Most criticism demoralizes, deflates, and discourages people from moving forward. Instead of motivating, it paralyzes. Instead of helping, it crushes a person's spirit and can significantly reduce a person's self-esteem.

Choice Theory teaches that to get what you want, you make your best attempt with the information available to you at that point in time. Pause for a moment and ask, "How is beating myself up for doing my best at the time helping me meet my need for Significance"?

Hindsight always provides information unavailable to you at the time of decision. You are not responsible for unavailable information, but you are responsible if you were aware more information was necessary and you failed to try and get it.

Creating guilt, anger, frustration, disappointment, or depression over past choices is incredibly unproductive. It won't bring you closer to the relationship you want to have with your Self, and it certainly won't help you move toward what you really want. In fact, you may end up feeling as though you don't deserve what you want.

Ask yourself, "Would I criticize my best friend for using the same behavior I just did to reach her goals and dreams?" If not, stop criticizing yourself. Accept responsibility without the blame and judgment.

Everyone wants to gain more control in their life. The process for getting there includes the following steps:

1. Relinquish the desire to control things over which you have no control.
2. Be present by refusing to worry about the future or regret your past.
3. Respond proactively instead of reacting to the actions of others.
4. Choose the choice that will best help you get what you want and accept responsibility for those choices.
5. Create the life you want.

Having a healthy relationship with control means you relinquish the desire to make others do things your way. As much as possible, keep your focus on being present in the here-and-now. You quickly respond to situations proactively to get what you want. You choose everything you do because you *want* to do it. And finally, with clarity, you will create what you want in your life. Let's delve more deeply into that process.

STEP ONE: RELINQUISH

"Peace is the result of retraining your mind to process life as it is, rather than as you think it should be." – Wayne Dyer

Give up the need to make others do things your way. When you claim the right to make your own decisions without the influence of others, it is only right that you extend this same courtesy. You have every right to ask for what you want from others. If you want to go on vacation with your best friend, ask, but if he or she declines your invitation, let it go. You have options! Go by yourself, stay home, or find someone else to go with you. There are always choices but, when working on a better relationship with your Self, don't chose nagging, begging, or bribing your friend into doing what he or she really doesn't want to do.

Another premise of Choice Theory is that you cannot escape an initial judgment; it is a natural response to new information. Your system determines whether it is positive, negative, or neutral as it compares the information to what you want in your Quality World. As you know from Chapter One, the Quality World is defined as your ideal world. New information will either match what you want, go against what you want, or have no negligible effect either way.

Letting go of controlling others will lead you to letting go of judging them, too. Have you ever had a friend who you think drinks too much and acts inappropriately when inebriated? This judgment happens regardless of your preference to not have it happen. The next step is to accept what has happened, but this doesn't mean you have to agree or approve of it. You simply accept that it's happened and isn't within your power to control or change. Remind yourself that your friend has every right to drink as much as he or she wants.

It's unlikely you have the power or control to make your friend stop, and silently disapproving while being judgmental of his or her behavior is not helping you have a positive relationship with control, with your friend, or with your Self. With all this in mind, make a decision about how much time you want to spend with this person when alcohol is involved.

STEP TWO: BE PRESENT

When you are truly present, you don't spend inordinate amounts of time ruminating over the past or worrying about what might happen in the future. Zen Master, Thich Nhat Hanh, says, "The most precious gift we can offer others is our presence. When mindfulness embraces those we love, they will bloom like flowers."

Studying the past holds two points of value. The past can reveal how to prevent negative occurrences in the future. Spanish philosopher, George Santayana, says, "Those who cannot remember the past are condemned to repeat it." Examining the past can also remind or allow you to discover your strengths. Traits or characteristics you used to get through a difficult period may be just what you need in your current situation.

When you're making an effort to be fully present but find yourself thinking about decisions you made in the past, simply remind yourself you did the best you could with what was available to you at the time. As already established in Chapter Two, all events in our lives have equal positive and negative value. When you are thinking of an event or decision negatively, search for and uncover the positives of that decision. You already know there are positives; you simply need to find them. Once you have, you will be able to release the regrets and return your focus to the present.

Time is your most valuable resource, and you waste it when you worry about the future. However, preparation for the future can be a productive thing. I have a friend that was greatly affected by Hurricane Katrina. As a result, he now has a "go bag" filled with everything he believes he will need in the event of a similar emergency. He learned what is possible and prepared for that possibility, freeing himself from worry. If your concern for the future involves something inevitable, out of your control, and impossible to prepare for, then your best bet for reducing anxiety is working on accepting what's coming.

Spending precious time regretting and worrying may be easier than taking steps to improve your situation. Change requires effort, and it can be scary. When you use regret and worry as excuses to keep you paralyzed and unable to act, nothing changes; you don't have to *do* anything. However, when you are ready to increase your level of Significance, you will ask yourself if there is anything you can do to improve the situation. If there is, then do it, and if not, return your thoughts to what is happening in the present. It's really all any of us have.

STEP THREE: RESPOND

Responding proactively requires you to recognize where you are and compare it to where you want to be, then determine which option will best help you reach your goal. You stop focusing on what you cannot change—you *act* instead of *react*. You accept the current reality as something that has occurred and cannot be changed; instead of wasting time reacting to circumstances, work to move forward to what you want rather than back to where you were before it happened.

When external obstacles present themselves, determine whether or not there is anything you can responsibly do to change the situation. If there is, use your influence to shape the situation. If there isn't, then accept it as a new part of your reality and move on. Here, "responsibly" means to meet your needs without preventing others from meeting theirs. It's not responsible to believe you have the right or duty to guide, cajole, guilt, coerce or control others into doing what you think is best. These behaviors usually result in harming, rather than helping, the relationship.

STEP FOUR: CHOOSE

How many things in your life do you tell yourself you do because you *have* to? There used to be an expression, "The only thing you have to do is die and pay taxes," but I know plenty of people who don't pay their taxes! As far as I'm concerned, the only thing you *have* to do is die eventually. Everything else is a choice.

When you have a dishonest relationship with control,

you believe much of what you do is forced upon you. You may talk about hating your job but *having* to go to work, not wanting to but *having* to pay the bills, or being unhappy in a relationship but *having* to stay. The truth is you do not have to go to work, pay your bills, or stay in an unhappy relationship. You choose to because of the benefits.

Anything you do is because you *want* to. You choose to work so you can provide for yourself and your family. You choose to pay your bills because you want electricity and water. You choose to stay in an unhappy relationship for many reasons— loyalty, fear, finances, religion, love, promises made, etc. When you get in touch with the reason you are doing what you believe you *have* to do, you will realize why you are choosing to do it.

If it sounds like semantics, it is because these semantics make all the difference. Consider the energy differential when you believe you *have* to do something versus you *want* to do something.

Try this over the next twenty-four hours. As you tune in to the language you use, see if you notice yourself using the words, "must" or "have to." You might hear yourself saying, "I *have* to go to the grocery store; I *have* to get the laundry done; I *must* finish this project." Take a breath, regroup, and playfully reframe to, "I'm grocery shopping to buy the foods I like in order to nourish those I love; I do the laundry so my family and I will get to feel our best wearing our favorite clothes; I want to finish this project so I can move on to what's next." This simple shift can take you from the victim to the victor, feeling more empowered and significant as you go.

STEP FIVE: CREATE

Having a healthy relationship with control will provide clarity in discovering what you want out of any situation. You are working to control yourself and letting go of the need to control others. Once you achieve that clarity, you begin to develop the positive relationship you crave with your Self and, consequently, with the other important people in your life. You come to believe you actually deserve what you want, and when that occurs, you can let yourself dream. As you gain specificity on what you want in your life, create it. Think about it, imagine it, talk about it, and seek out those who can be resources as you move toward your goals.

Living this way leaves little time for focusing on what doesn't serve the manifestation of what you want in your life. You won't spend time plotting and planning how to get people to do what you want, regretting situations of the past, making excuses for why you can never have what you want, or fearing the accomplishment of your dreams. You will be much too busy creating opportunities for success to waste your time on those choices.

Relationship with Your Inherent Value and Worth

"We can only be said to be alive in those moments when our hearts are conscious of our treasure." – Thornton Wilder

I suspect if you are reading this book, you have had some challenges believing that you have high value and worth. You probably think there are many people "better" than you. The goal of this chapter is to help you acknowledge your true value and worth.

I had a mother who constantly told me, "Kimberly, you are no better than anyone else but no one else is any better than you either." This is one of those early childhood messages that didn't serve me very well. I always had a drive to do my best, but when I exceeded others' efforts or accomplishments, I felt guilty. I attempted to hide my gifts, talents, and abilities so I didn't seem like I was better than anyone else.

I now understand what my mother tried to tell me. In fact, there is a lot of wisdom in what she said; it was my interpretation of her message that created conflict. A neurosurgeon is no better than a store clerk, and a CEO no better than a janitor. Every single human being has equal value and worth by virtue of the fact that they are here and breathing. You compromise a healthy relationship with your Self when you perceive yourself as either better or worse than anyone else. By virtue of being alive, you have the value everyone else does.

When young children discover themselves in a mirror, they delight in what they see and are empowered by the fact that their movements are being mimicked. This reflects self-love and mastery.

Experiencing an incident of self-love and mastery is a pure moment of positive self-evaluation. You're not comparing yourself to someone else, trying to decide if you're better or worse, or consulting anyone else's opinion. Instead, you are enamored with your Self, understanding and appreciating your own value and worth.

Throughout life, relationships and experiences will either help improve your level of self-esteem or exacerbate it. Many factors contribute to how you see yourself, but most of them ignore your inner voice and rely on the opinions of others; you determine your value and worth based on how they see you. Other people's perceptions of you have absolutely nothing to do with your inherent value and worth.

This is often underscored by the "isms" of the world—sexism, racism, ageism, etc. and other groups that are discriminated against, such as homosexuals, transgendered individuals, Jews, Muslims, lower socioeconomic groups, etc. When you belong to a group that is considered a minority or non-dominant culture, you may value yourself less based upon discrimination, negative stereotyping and the treatment you receive from the dominant culture. You could also take that discrimination and use it as motivation to prove the dominant culture wrong by accepting and owning your inherent value and worth. These things, from the earliest perception of power differentials, create the tendency to focus more on the greater society's valuing of you as a member of the discriminated group than your own inner knowing and self-evaluation.

The perception that you have lesser value because of your membership in any group you belong to is simply a lie. This misinformation may be perpetuated by the media, government and the dominant culture. If this is your struggle, it might be helpful to remember what life was like for you before you became aware of any power differential. Remember or imagine yourself as the infant in love with your reflection in the mirror. At a young age, you understood your value and worth until an inequitable environment wore you down and convinced you that your inner knowing was somehow wrong. Reclaim your positive self-worth based on the fact that you are here and breathing. You have just as much worth as anyone else—not more, not less.

When you accept that everything you experience has equal positive and negative value, you realize people who do bad things provide their victims with lessons and opportunities, as long as they are willing to find and accept them. Thus, even people who do horrible things are adding something positive into the world. This is a perspective that is challenging to get to but is completely freeing and empowering when embraced.

Your self-worth is also shaped by how much you contribute to "the greater good." Who can know what the greater good of humanity is without the gift of hindsight? Who should have the final say in its definition? If you adhere to your own self-determination of your value and worth, then the only person who can assess whether or not you are contributing to the greater good is you. Your self-esteem will be higher when you believe you are acting in a way, small or large, that benefits humanity.

When you accept that everyone, in terms of value, is created equally, then your determination of how valuable you see yourself follows. The question becomes how well are you maximizing the personal gifts you were given for the betterment of humanity?

Naturally, there will be different opinions about what constitutes the betterment of humanity but, since we are talking about *self*-worth, it is *your* opinion that matters. If you know you are using, developing, and sharing your gifts for the good of humankind, then you will have a stronger sense of self-worth. Conversely, you will perceive your value to be lower if you believe there is nothing special about you, you know your gifts and ignore them, or you knowingly use your uniqueness against the greater good.

Once at the original Yankee Stadium during a game, I needed to use the restroom and wasn't looking forward to the experience. I know how dirty those places can be, particularly during a time many people are using them. Imagine my surprise when I walked in and the place was pristine. The cleaning person was in there scrubbing counters and mopping floors. I was so happy with the condition of this public restroom that I said to the woman, "Thank you so much for what you do. This bathroom is so clean, it's a pleasure to use it." The woman beamed. It was obvious she was used to doing her job and being invisible.

Her gift may be the ability and desire to make things sparkly clean, and she is using that gift to help others. Imagine if she didn't do her job well, there could be countless germs to contract. Not doing her job well could result in illness and possibly even death. Her contribution is extremely important to the people she serves.

Your heart surgeon is only as good as the cleanliness of his or her instruments. Who is more important, the doctor or the person who sterilizes the surgical tools? Both are critical to a successful operation.

SELF-ESTEEM

Everyone's value and worth is equal; there is something you are supposed to contribute to others. Your gifts, talents, and abilities are not just for you—they are meant to be shared.

The first step is to find out your strengths. What do you love? What do you get involved with and lose track of time doing? When do you feel like you're in "the zone," that place where things happen effortlessly?

When I get immersed in a meaningful conversation with someone, I lose time. When I'm speaking to an audience, sometimes the words seem to come from outside myself. I have similar experiences when writing. Without a conscious thought, phrases and sentences appear on the screen! When I am in the zone, things happen that help people.

If I were writing and keeping it to myself, I would not be living up to my potential, and my self-esteem would diminish through my unwillingness to share my gifts with the world. The world needs my help in the areas I have help to give, just like it needs your help. When I believe I'm not important and what I have to contribute doesn't matter, I rob others of my gifts.

I'm not saying I have something phenomenal to contribute to every human on the planet. What I have to share won't resonate with everyone, but unless I risk and put myself out there, no one will benefit and I wouldn't be living up to my potential.

Does this make me better than anyone else? Of course not. Your self-esteem is not measured by *what* you do, but by your willingness to share your gifts, talents, and abilities with the people who want and need them. If I knew I had a message to share but was discouraged by how difficult it would be, how others may not like it, or how insignificant I am, then my self-esteem would be damaged.

Not everyone is aware of their special strengths. Perhaps you were told you were worthless early in life and you believed it. Maybe you think there's nothing special about you because you were told you are no better than anyone else, like my mother told me. Perhaps you think everyone can do the things you do and that your gifts are nothing significant. While it's true you are not any better than anyone else, it is also true that you have unique gifts, talents, and abilities you are supposed to discover, develop, and deploy for the greater good.

Here's how you can establish and maintain a healthy level of self-esteem:

1. Believe you have inherent value and worth by virtue of the simple fact of being.
2. Believe you have unique gifts, talents, and abilities to claim.
3. Accept and know what your strengths are.
4. Work on further crafting your skills.
5. Use and share your gifts, talents, and abilities with others to promote the greater good of humankind.

6. Stay on the lookout for lessons to help you get even better.

If you already implement these steps in your life, then you probably have a healthy level of self-esteem. If your self-esteem could stand improvement, please read on.

You have inherent value and worth by virtue of the simple fact of being.

When you were born, you had unlimited potential. You were a living, breathing example of all that could be—then you began to live your life. Many things have contributed to the person you are today. You had caregivers, early childhood experiences, and education to list a few. Some of your experiences were excellent, some average, and some poor or even horrific. Because of your experiences, you either found it easy, average or difficult to believe in your inherent value and worth.

Whatever your previous thinking, know that those people who didn't support you in the past were doing the best they knew how in their own lives and circumstances; they were limited and you may have suffered because of it.

For your own benefit, it is critical to forgive them so you can move forward with what was intended for you either before, in spite of, or even because of what happened. Sometimes, life's worst experiences provide you with the opportunity to help others going through similar challenges. Don't waste the opportunity by staying stuck in victimhood. There are others going through similar things who need you now, and there are things you can do for them. You are significant. You have wisdom to share. You matter!

CLAIM YOUR UNIQUE GIFTS, TALENTS, AND ABILITIES

It is not uncommon for people to be unaware of their unique gifts, talents, and abilities because they take them for granted. One of my strengths is the ability to form meaningful relationships with others. I have the ability to find things in most people I like and respect, see their potential for greatness, and provide a safe space for people to share personal information.

I have been aware of this raw skill since fifth grade, but I didn't think it was anything special. I thought everyone could do it.

I have a friend who has the most beautiful baritone voice, and he didn't realize how special it is until later in life. He assumed everyone could sing and that his voice was nothing special. Another person I know bakes pies in bulk; she thinks nothing of making thirty pies at one time. And then, you know what she does? She gives them away! When I told her this was a gift of hers, she brushed it off by saying anyone could do it. "Not so," I said. "And even if everyone could, you are the one who does." She discounts the special talent she possesses, robbing her of a real sense of her own self-worth.

If it feels arrogant or boastful to think of your strengths, please imagine what the world would be like if you rob it of what you have to offer. These strengths are bigger than you—they are about the good you can do for others. If a man, who owns a boat, rescues drowning people, would it be arrogant because he has a boat and they don't? Or is he being helpful by using his assets for the greater good? What do you have to offer that other people might need?

ENUMERATE YOUR STRENGTHS

Take inventory of your strengths. When I was in high school, I was good at math. For a brief time, I thought I might become a math teacher. I also realized religion was important to me so, for another short period of time, I considered becoming a missionary. On top of that, I had a strong desire to travel and contemplated being a flight attendant. It's interesting, but not at all surprising, that I have combined all those strengths into what I call my life, which is the expression of my unique gifts, talents, and abilities. I am a public speaker who engages with her audiences, using my relationship-building skills. What I talk about is highly spiritual, though not religious. The work I do enables me to travel, and I use my math skills in the daily operation of my business.

It is important to know your strengths so you can cultivate them. How can you care for something when you don't know what it is?

There are other obstacles that may hold you back from realizing your potential. For example, a natural mountain climber who lives in a flat area may never realize his strength. However, if it is a strength that will assist others, opportunities for exposure will likely arise—you just have to choose them. It will require surrendering to the path that opens up for you.

You may also be limited by the societal rules and customs of where you live. There are places women are not permitted certain privileges men take for granted. There are areas where privilege is awarded based on skin color, language, religion, intelligence, and net worth. You may not see a way to access things denied to you, but if you have a gift, it will demand expression in some way.

Learn what your strengths are, and explore them. Ask others to share what they see in you. Expose yourself to new experiences so you can discover things about your Self. Make a list to later see if you can incorporate them into your life, while serving the highest good.

DEVELOP YOUR SKILLS

Having a strength is a gift. You can take that gift and put it in your piggy bank where it can't grow, or you can invest it in a way that causes it to grow exponentially. The choice is yours, and being clear about your strengths allows you to make that informed decision.

When you share a strength with others, it is prudent to develop that strength so you can be as competent at it as possible. Perhaps you fear it's narcissistic to focus on developing your skill and becoming great at what you do. Instead, see it as a debt you owe to the people you serve. Through maximizing your value and worth, you become the vessel for divine expression to manifest.

People started coming to me to talk about their problems when I was ten years old. My fellow students talked to me about drama with their crushes, fights they were having with their friends, and restrictions placed on them by their parents. I was in fifth grade and already was "helping" people with relationship problems!

I don't remember much of what I did or said, but I am convinced I've honed my craft since then, continuing to practice with anyone who asks for my help. I went to college for psychology and worked with schizophrenics in the community. Five years later, I worked with physically, sexually, and emotionally abused children and their families. I eventually got my master's degree in Counseling. After specializing in Choice Theory/Reality Therapy, I became a trainer for William Glasser International. Now I'm a board certified coach and complete my continuing education credits each year. I strive to always improve what I do by practicing and living these concepts in my own life.

When you're just coasting with your gift, you will know there is more you could be doing to improve. To move closer to integrity with your Self, frequently ask, "What am I doing to get better at what I do best?"

AVOID COMPARISONS

At some point in life, you stop using your internal navigation system and start looking to others for direction. You don't trust your Self to evaluate how you are doing in your growth and development.

No one else can know where you're supposed to be in life. You have your own GPS, and only you can know your true direction. Of course, ask for others' advice. It is acceptable and even advisable to seek the opinions of others, not for ultimate answers but to gather more information before making your own decisions.

You might seek the opinions of people who have already accomplished what you are attempting to do. You may have mentors and trusted advisors in your life. You could hire personal coaches to help you move to the next level in your life, but only you can truly know and choose the direction you will take. Subjugating this responsibility to another person will negatively affect the relationship you have with yourself.

It is also counterproductive to measure your progress based on where others are. Being *the* best is not as important as being *your* best. When you struggle to be the best, any sense of accomplishment will be short-lived. Being recognized as the "best" requires constant defense, because everyone else is striving to become better than you.

Change can sometimes be immediate but often it is a process; be patient with yourself. Improvements do not happen overnight. Measure your progress not only from yesterday, but also from where you began, to recognize how far you've come.

You can always get better than you were the day before. Striving to be the best you can be can result in others recognizing you as *the* "best," but your motivation for getting there was not to defeat anyone. You did not achieve your success through someone else's failure, but you used your own GPS to direct you toward constant improvement. You're honing the gift you can offer to the world. You owe it to your Self, as well as them, to consistently be better than you were the last time.

I recently saw a magazine that named an athlete turned actor as the "Sexiest Man Alive." I had a laugh and wondered who the judges were because I did not agree. Realize that everyone's taste is different, and being your best may not align with the popular opinion of "the best." Having a healthy relationship with your value and worth will see you comparing only to *your* last best, not to someone else's definition of *the* "best." When you are being your best, the right people will be attracted to your energy. It may or may not be what attracts the masses, but it will attract those who will benefit from your particular talents.

SHARE YOUR SKILLS FOR THE GREATER GOOD

Most people intuitively know if they are on a path of enlightenment or a path of destruction, but there are definitely some gray areas. For example, take a world leader and a gang leader—both use similar gifts and skills. While the world leader may be doing what he or she believes will better humankind, the gang leader is focused more on what will benefit himself and his followers, not necessarily the public good.

Consider Adolph Hitler and Mahatma Gandhi—both used their gifts and strengths and believed they were acting in the world's best interests. The results are far different. Based on historical accounts, Hitler believed that slaughtering millions of innocent people would save Germany by creating a master race, helping those who belonged to it. He believed he was using his gifts for the greater good, and therefore may have had a high sense of self-worth. Gandhi, on the other hand, had a strong sense of humility; he understood everyone is equal and he was no better than anyone else. He used his gifts to serve the greater good without needing praise or accolades from others. He had a calling and rose to the occasion.

ALWAYS LOOK FOR LESSONS THAT HELP YOU IMPROVE

Using your talents to help others leads you to a desire to improve. You will want to hone your skills so you can be of better service to even more people. Part of maximizing your value is to remain teachable so you become a lifelong learner. Watch and learn from others who are good at what you do, and seek out mentors who can help you reach new levels. You will not be content staying where you are. Tune into your inner knowing for self-evaluation, and your need for Significance will drive you to improve.

Generally, the happiest person has a healthy recognition of self-worth without an inflated view of his or her importance. There is a fine line between confidence and arrogance, but confidence will serve you better. Confidence implies a certain sense of surety and worth, while recognizing that you are a very small part of an enormous world. No one person is any more important than anyone else.

Think of self-worth as a spectrum. At one end are those who are arrogant, recognizing their own self-worth but looking down upon those they deem unworthy. At the other end, there are those who recognize the importance of others but don't believe they are worthy to even breathe air. In the middle of the spectrum, you'll find people with a healthy balance of self-worth. The sweet spot is confidence without arrogance and the knowledge you are good enough, but no better than anyone else.

Healthy levels of self-esteem and self-respect are crucial in having a positive relationship with your inherent value and worth. Self-esteem requires feeling good about who you are and liking yourself. Self-respect is about seeing yourself as valuable, providing something important to others. Do you realize how important you are?

RELATIONSHIP WITH YOUR PASSION

"And as we let our own light shine, we unconsciously give other people the permission to do the same. As we're liberated from our own fear, our presence automatically liberates others." – Marianne Williamson

While I was in Cabo writing this book, a middle-aged man spoke to another woman and I about his passion. He loves to cook, but isn't employed as a chef because he can't afford to make only fifteen dollars an hour. He got into construction for the fifty an hour pay rate so he could have more for his life. The woman was agreeing with him, claiming you can't always make a living doing what you love. She admitted she loves crafts but is a supervisor of an IT group; it pays her health insurance and allowed her to send her children to college. I brought up exclusive chefs who are in high demand, and while he agreed those people exist, he wasn't willing to put in the years of practice for the unfavorable pay. Instead, what I heard in his voice was the disbelief that he would never be good enough to become one of those elite chefs. When I asked the woman if she could imagine putting her hobbies to use, she laughed and said it would never pay the bills.

I felt sad both of them shared that opinion. If I were their coach, I would be asking them some very different questions. I believe he could become a highly acclaimed master chef and she could make a fortune putting her craft skills to use in service of others. Living without a healthy sense of purpose can lead you to live a life of mediocrity. You could live a life that falls far short of what could be for yourself and for the others you would touch by living your purpose.

Both of those people knew their passion and chose to dabble in it in their spare time, within the confines of their own homes. He sometimes creatively cooks new dishes for himself and his fiancé and she makes homemade craft projects as gifts for special occasions. Both get joy from doing so but they are not blessing others with their passion to the extent they could be.

Many people are uncertain of their passion. My niece is twenty-three, has graduated college, and has many passions. She is a singer, instrumentalist, and a writer. She loves hoop dance, wants to travel, and has a strong affinity for political activism. She is young and still exploring her interests. However, it's never too early to start thinking about combining your interests in a way that serves others while giving you a truly unique life.

I have a friend who loves to sing, entertain, and deliver empowering messages through public speaking. He turns public speaking into a production for the delight of his audiences and himself; he often sings his messages to the audience. He combines his passions to create a truly unique experience for his audiences and has work he loves to do!

Are there people who truly don't know their passion? I believe it's possible, but it's more likely they are devaluing what they are good at. The sad irony is that these gifts shine like beacons in the night for others to see, but the owners can't see them for themselves. Others can recognize your gift when you don't think it's anything special.

If you are thinking, *I don't fit into any of the above categories. I just don't know what my passion is,* there are three additional possibilities:

1. There's so much self-depreciating, negative chatter going on in your head that you can't hear your own true voice and are immobilized by pain.
2. You have not been exposed to things that will uncover your passion.
3. You have accepted someone else's version of what

your passion is supposed to be and it isn't in sync with your own.

The solutions are as follows:

1. You read about what to do in Chapter Two. Listen closely to the negative self-talk in your head and identify it as content to critically examine. Determine the veracity of that content, thank the voice for its concern, and dismiss it as you would if someone told you the sky is green and the grass is blue. It's so obviously untrue, it doesn't require one more moment of your time, energy, or consideration.

2. If someone is born with a passion for downhill skiing but has never seen a slope, then that person is lacking exposure. If someone is an amazing dancer but was born into a family that said dancing is a sin, that person would also lack exposure. You must break away from the physical or emotional restraints that prevent you from responding to the inner push that's trying to shove you toward where you belong. Trust your Self and move toward your bliss.

3. Some people are told what they are to become. I knew a person with a certain passion for law enforcement, but his father had lived through the Great Depression; he believed if those conditions ever reoccurred, an auto mechanic would always have work. This man lived the life his father chose for him, and he died wondering what could have been had he walked his own path.

By all means, listen to outside opinions, particularly from those you love, trust, and respect. Compare their advice to your inner knowing. Does it make sense, feel right, and sound like something you want to do? Can you see yourself satisfied in the life that's being proposed? If yes, explore the option; if not, thank them for their concern and go down the path you believe will lead you to the life you're destined to create for your own happiness and the well-being of others.

In writing this section, I remembered a conversation I had when I was getting ready to go to college for psychology. I was seventeen years-old and had known since fifth grade that I wanted to help people with their problems. One day, my mother and I were having a conversation and she told me, "Why would you want to go into psychology? You will never make any money at it." I listened, I heard her, and my naïve reply was, "Everything isn't about money for me."

My mother was initially right; I didn't make any money when I started. It was 1982, the US national average wage index for that year was $14,531, and my first job paid $7,000/year—pretty unimpressive. Because I was good at what I did, I earned a promotion within two months and made $9,000/year. Five years later, I took a new job at a foster care agency where I stayed for the next seventeen years. Many promotions later, I was the Director of Training & Development. My new position morphed into my passion. That is when my passion transformed from counseling and supervision to training counselors. I hadn't had the exposure to know that was something I loved, but once I discovered that passion, things really expanded for me.

In 2004, I left the foster care agency, moved to Chicago, and opened my own speaking, coaching and consulting business. Coaching for Excellence made it through the first year despite only making $30,000. Its income has quadrupled since then and is still climbing. It's all because I followed my passion. Neither my mother nor I could have ever anticipated this business growth, but it naturally happens when you are following your passion and genuinely serving others.

Financially successful people can serve others by donating money and employing people. I am so happy I'm in a position where I'm able to build a team of people I employ, expanding my reach to help even more people. The Law of Reciprocity is about giving and receiving, and it's truly amazing how it has expanded my business and life. I used to be a giver that blocked others from giving to me. I believed I was better off than most, so I should do the giving. I came to realize how arrogant that was. While I was giving and feeling so good about it, I was preventing others from having that same awesome feeling. It was selfish. By receiving, I was providing a spiritual pathway for others to feel good and to receive in return, then more came back to me. This was not the purpose for doing it, though, it was a consequence. My purpose was very clear—I wanted to provide others the opportunity to give. It yields such wonderful benefits.

I no longer think of money as the curse I once thought it was. I don't think of wealthy people as snobby and selfish anymore. I believe there are all types of people with money, just as there are all types of people without it. Money is a means of currency—that's all. It's what you choose to do with it that determines the type of person you are.

I have also learned to define wealth more broadly these days. For some, wealth means having a lot of money, investments, and freedom to do whatever they want whenever they want. However, there are many other kinds of wealth. People who have both quality and quantity of meaningful relationships are wealthy. People can have wealth in terms of the work they do, being willing to do their work for free because it brings them so much joy. People who are certain of their place in the Universe are wealthy in spirituality. People who are able to do what they want without concern for the opinions of others are wealthy in freedom. There are so many ways to define wealth and to be wealthy. What is your definition? Do you consider yourself a wealthy person?

To reach your wealth, develop your inner knowing to recognize your passion. Find a way to do it every day while blessing others with the fruits of your labor which, of course, isn't labor at all to you. When you are operating in your bliss, you lose time. You get in the zone and you do what brings you joy. How can this be called work? It is only called work by those who do not understand and who have not experienced being in their zone, fueled by passion as they serve others.

Leave Your Legacy

Amassing huge amounts of money is a passion for some, and the reality of not being able to take it with you can present either a frustration or an opportunity. For many with great financial wealth, they plan estates that can take care of families, provide charity for personal causes, or build wings at hospitals or universities bearing their name. These are just some of the opportunities that exist for those with fortunes. But in case you are not one of those mega billionaires, what will be your legacy?

Thinking about your death is not the easiest thing to do. The thought is unpleasant and, for many, fraught with uncertainty. And yet, lying on your deathbed, you will find satisfaction in leaving something valuable behind, something that will represent you into eternity.

Relational

One way to measure your legacy is through the people you have touched. For some, one's legacy is their children and their children's children. Having another person on the planet that has half your DNA can be the most satisfying thing ever and cannot be minimized. I have two sons I am extremely proud of and seven beautiful grandchildren that will carry on my legacy long into the future. When comprehending the reach of your relational legacy, everything you do, everything your children do, and their children do, and their children's children do started with you and even those that came before you. This is an extremely comforting thought to me as I age.

People can also leave relational legacies having nothing to do with familial ties. We leave behind people whose lives we have touched, not just our family members. What relational legacy are you cultivating?

TANGIBLE

Another way to measure your legacy is by the outcomes you have produced. By the time you are reading this book, I will have written three books, a parenting curriculum for court-mandated parents, and a board certified coaching program. I am proud of these creations, and they will be part of my tangible legacy that hopefully will be enjoyed for years to come. My father-in-law built buildings and bridges. My father was a land developer. Artists, song writers, and actors leave their mark in a tangible way. There are multiple ways to leave tangible legacies. What will yours be?

INTANGIBLE

You can also measure your legacy by the people you've served. Some people have jobs where they save lives, heal the sick, teach, preach, protect, clean, and counsel. There is a relational factor in every job; it's possible for people to benefit from anything you can think to do. When thinking of your legacy, you can think about all the people that were helped by the work you do.

Perhaps my largest legacy to date are the countless people whose lives have been touched by things I have said and done—some of them I know, others I don't. I had the excellent fortune of learning the concepts of Choice Theory psychology, now the study and application of it my life's work, when I had just turned twenty-seven. The information contained within Choice Theory is so valuable, I find it impossible not to share. I have taught it directly to those asking to learn it and to those mandated to hear it, and I have taught it indirectly by demonstrating living with Choice Theory for anyone who has come into contact with me over the years.

I feel the need to print a disclaimer here: living with Choice Theory is a little like wearing the bracelet, WWJD (What would Jesus do?). It's an admirable goal to aspire to, but hardly one can perfectly achieve. There have been times in my life when I didn't embody the essence of Choice Theory, but it is always my aspiration to do so. Most of those who have been inspired by me recognize my intent; they know my heart, though not perfect, is always willing to improve.

When you operate in your passion, you cannot help but leave a legacy. It may not be the tangible kind, such as children, a building you had a hand in constructing, or a book you wrote, but there will always be the legacy of the lives you improved by operating in your passion in service of others. What will your legacy be? What will you leave behind to make the world a better place than when you first arrived?

If you want more Significance in your life, then be more significant. The need for Significance is about making a difference, having an impact, and leaving a legacy after you're gone. It is about respect. It is about being powerful. It doesn't require the approval or agreement of others. You have the internal GPS to know whether or not you are making a difference and having an impact. Significance isn't something you go out and get—significance is something you were born with. You simply need to remember and step into it.

What doesn't work:
1. Controlling other people.
2. Being a victim.
3. Criticizing yourself.
4. Worrying.
5. Thinking you do things because you *have* to.
6. Listening to the voices of others instead of your own.
7. Ignoring or taking your strengths for granted.
8. Comparing and competing with others.
9. Focusing on what's wrong with you.
10. Hating those areas that create pain for you.
11. Ceasing to learn.

What does:
1. Accepting others for who they are.
2. Taking responsibility for the things you do.
3. Encouraging yourself.
4. Trusting Divine order.
5. Realizing everything you do, you do because you *want* to.
6. Being present.
7. Hearing and following your own inner guidance system.
8. Noticing your flaws.
9. Noticing your best characteristics.
10. Competing with and improving yourself.
11. Focusing on what you like most.
12. Appreciating the parts of you that have been painful in the past.
13. Changing what you can for a better overall life
14. Recognizing and using your strengths to help others.
15. Forgiving yourself.
16. Becoming a lifelong learner.

FREEDOM

"Today I choose life. Every morning when I wake up I can choose joy, happiness, negativity, pain... To feel the freedom that comes from being able to continue to make mistakes and choices—today I choose to feel life, not to deny my humanity but embrace it." – Kevyn Aucoin

*A*re you someone who likes doing what you want more than almost anything else? Do you dislike being restricted or having limited options? Are you fiercely independent? Do you sometimes make a choice that's not in your best interest just to do the opposite of what someone told you to do? Do you prefer time alone over time with other people? Are you a person who deeply values privacy? Do you often question rules and fight against the status quo? Are you someone who values the ability to engage your creativity? Then you probably have a higher need for Freedom.

There are basically two types of freedom—there is *freedom from* weight, restriction, and control and there is the *freedom to* have the things you want, do the things you want, and be the person you want. Freedom encompasses both your physical and emotional freedom.

When you are low on Freedom, you may feel restricted, dependent, and controlled. If you're feeling any of these things, assess your current level of Freedom. You may be feeling antsy without realizing the source. Maybe you feel the need to break free *from* whatever is holding you back, or you may want to push through *to* the Freedom you want. How free are you feeling? Do you have exactly the right amount, not enough, or possibly too much?

Even with a lower need for Freedom, it can seem like a priority when it isn't being met. This can happen when you're inundated with people and a lack of privacy; perhaps you're experiencing people attempting to control you, or maybe you feel trapped without any decent options. There are a number of scenarios that will cause your Freedom need to push for greater satisfaction. It's not that the need has grown stronger, you are just having a more difficult time meeting it.

Having more Freedom than you need may cause you to feel adrift and somewhat unsafe, unsure of your boundaries. You may be feeling disconnected from important people in your life. With an abundance of Freedom, your level of independence may deter people from asking if you ever need help. This can lead to loneliness and a sense that you have no one to rely on other than yourself.

If you find yourself needing more Freedom in your life, what you can do depends on your situation. You can withdraw from the center of activity; if necessary, talk to the people close to you about needing space. You can question the rules that don't make sense and speak your mind about what you are thinking. Sometimes it's as simple as taking a day to do nothing other than exactly what you want, regardless of what others want *from* you.

Just like the needs mentioned previously, if what you need is Freedom, no amount of Safety & Security, Significance, Connection or Joy will satisfy. Only freedom can satisfy Freedom.

This may sound like an oxymoron for those with high Freedom needs, but you may have some rules about Freedom. Those with a higher need for Freedom typically abhor rules, particularly the ones that don't seem to make sense, but the rules I'm talking about are more subconscious and self-imposed. Some examples are refusing to ask for help, opposing authority whether or not it makes sense, and withdrawing and isolating yourself more than is comfortable.

Perception always plays an important role in everything. You may steer clear from something you perceive to threaten your Freedom, but with a simple tweak of your perception, you can experience that same thing as something that satisfies your Freedom need. For example, eating whatever you want may feel freeing, but it can result in poor health, making it harder to move and exert energy. Tweaking that perception can help you see that regular exercise and healthy eating will provide the long-term Freedom you actually need.

Limiting beliefs may be creating challenges for you. You may believe you don't deserve Freedom, which usually takes the form of perceived obligations, guilt, or safety needs. You may not exercise your Freedom because there are people who need you; you don't want to attend to their needs, but you limit yourself by believing you have no choice. Guilt can destroy your freedom because you come to believe for whatever reason, you don't deserve it. You may resist vocational Freedom by convincing yourself that you need the regular paycheck, healthcare, or vacation time.

When I think of Freedom, I think of independence, creativity, and the ability to make choices. It is about freeing ourselves from what holds us back and soaring to the heights we choose. When you are free, you are in control of your own life, and no person or circumstance can dictate what is best for you.

I discovered an important area of Freedom through remodeling my living space. You need to be able to create a space for yourself where you feel safe, nurtured, powerful, joyful, and free. This may not seem like Freedom to you, but it satisfied my Freedom in regard to choice, creativity, and the ability to create a space that is completely mine, without interference. I call this Freedom with your environment.

The next section covers freedom from self-created misery. No one likes to be miserable, and most people believe misery is created by things beyond their control. The reality is that misery is self-inflicted. When you are in control, it's much easier to accomplish freedom from misery.

The final area we will address is the ultimate component to Freedom: the freedom to be yourself. Throughout your life, you play roles. You start out as someone's son or daughter, become a friend, a cousin, a sister or brother, a mother or father, a student, an employee and a myriad of other roles. But who are you? Are you free enough to explore that question? Do you have the freedom to be your Self?

RELATIONSHIP WITH YOUR ENVIRONMENT

"I think the home should rise up and greet you." – Nate Berkus

When I initially moved to Chicago, I rented a condo from a friend who wanted to move to California indefinitely. I got a place to live, and he had the comfort of knowing someone he trusted was taking care of his home; here I've been for twelve years.

For the first five years, I used things that were his; I wasn't disturbing his space in case he returned, and it kept me from having to spend money. Over in California, my friend got a good job and a wife, and the likelihood of him returning to Chicago became quite slim. I asked if he would consider selling his condo to me and he was happy to take my offer—I became a homeowner again. While I wanted to remodel and make the home more mine, I first needed to improve my credit score; going further into debt was not on my agenda. I kept using his things, left his artwork on the wall, threw some paint on the walls and continued living my life.

The other thing that happened was more insidious— my condo was more of an office than a home. I didn't invite people over. I never entertained. The space was great for me, a single woman who worked a lot from home, but it wasn't really conducive to living a full life. A friend of mine came to visit me and stayed at my place. After being there a couple of days, she said, "Kim, I don't see you in this space. Where is Kim?" I was so much in denial, I didn't even know what she was talking about at that time.

I told another close friend of mine about this comment and how I didn't understand what she meant. My friend said, "Well, Kim, you don't really *live* there; you *work* there." It took me a moment before I realized exactly what she was talking about. I couldn't remember the last time I ate at home. Yes, I traveled a lot and ate out all the time while on the road, but I kept that habit while I was home, too! I convinced myself there was no time to grocery shop and cook, especially since I would only be home a week before leaving again. My kitchen table was covered with stacks of papers necessary for my variety of unfinished projects, which I always wanted to be visible so I wouldn't forget about them. My living room was no different; my couch was filled with papers because I enjoyed working there, feet up and television on. Oh yeah, and did I mention my spare bedroom? It's an office with a big desk, filing cabinet, and futon that are all overflowing with work items.

Not even my bedroom was safe from my work. On the days I don't have to leave the house, I work in bed until lunch time. I had to ask myself, "Is this a problem? What does this say about me?"

After much soul-searching, I realized my surroundings were great to work in, as comfort is all I require, but they were not healthy for my personal life. I was subconsciously avoiding using my space for anything personal, and that realization was an eye opener for me. A big part of taking care of yourself is creating a space that nurtures you, fills your heart, and feels like home. I didn't have that. For twelve years, that was something I was missing, maybe even craving, but because my relationship wasn't right with my finances, I believed I had to deprive myself of a nurturing environment. I didn't have the freedom with my environment I needed.

About two months after I wrote the financial section of this book, I got a call from my girlfriend whose husband does some contracting work. We had talked about the renovations I wanted to make, and how I envisioned it happening over a five-year period to spread out the financial commitment of such a large project. When my girlfriend told me her husband was ready to work, I felt the universe usher me closer to having a loving relationship with myself. My contractor was ready, I was ready, and my wallet was ready. After finishing the kitchen, he replaced a wall with tacky mirrored tiles from the seventies with fresh paint and a gorgeous, handcrafted oak bookshelf—I felt no shame in celebrating with my own tacky victory dance. He got rid of a loose piece of linoleum that plagued my laundry room and replaced it with beautiful black tile.

While my contractor began the work, he was offered a promotion… in Tennessee! Did I mention I was in Chicago? Though he said he could finish the work before leaving, it threw my five-year plan out the window. I was glad he could finish the work, but I felt more than a little pressure, all self-imposed, to come up with the money to create the home I really wanted.

Things took longer than expected, as they often do, and he left for Tennessee before getting to the bathroom that I wanted remodeled floor to ceiling. He didn't leave me without referring me to another contractor, and so began the second stage of me getting right with my environment. My home is totally remodeled now and I am proud of my surroundings. I have the freedom with my environment I wanted.

Creating an environment where you feel you truly belong is an essential part of taking care of yourself. There are no rules about what this looks like. It is about asking yourself, "Does this space, item, color, fabric call to me, bring me joy, nurture me, and feel like home?" You will know you have accomplished this goal when you have a place you *want* to be. You will miss it when you are away. You will want to share it with the important people in your life. When you have something to ponder, your thoughts flow freely in this space. When you are hurt or injured, you know it is a place you can heal. This can be inside your home, outside, or both. Now that I have this space, I can't even imagine what I was thinking or how I was managing without it. Becoming right with your environment wasn't even on my radar for the initial outline of this book, but since you're reading the section I've dedicated to it, it's obvious I've realized its importance.

I now have an environment I'm proud of; I believe my space is a beautiful expression of my personality. I love to entertain, but after a taxing day, I look forward to going home to relax. My home is comfortable, serviceable, practical, peaceful, and beautiful.

When you know you are worthy, you will create this space. If you live with others, claim a spot that is yours and allow your partner or roommate to do the same. It might be a room, an annex, or simply a corner, but create an environment just for you.

Creating the exact environment you want may be costly. If you are simultaneously working on your relationship with finances, like I was, then you may not be willing to completely create the environment you want right now. However, you can take small steps in that direction—buy a candle, a plant, organizing bins, window treatments, new hardware for your kitchen cupboards—anything that will give you a little lift while staying within your budget.

Create a list of what you ultimately want to do and, within your own time frame and budget, move toward your goals while increasing your financial freedom. I didn't do my major renovations until after my credit card debt was reduced. While I was waiting, it was helpful to imagine the things I planned to do when I was ready and, in the meantime, I purchased salt lamps, diffusers and essential oils, window treatments, and paint for my walls, all of which were within my budget until I could get to the bigger ticket items of remodeling my kitchen and bathroom.

Here are the steps:

1. Know where you are and be grateful for it.
2. Develop the vision of what your ideal environment looks like.
3. Take small steps in that direction while improving your relationship with your finances.
4. Make the big things happen when you are in a financial position to do so.

What do you want to do to improve your relationship with your environment?

Once you have created the freeing environment you want, maintaining it is important. When you are right with your environment, you won't allow piles of clothes, clutter, or crud to invade your space. Whether you do it yourself or hire someone else, having the environment you want comes with a maintenance contract you make with yourself.

I'm not saying you must become a slave to your surroundings. If cleaning is not your strength and seems to drain you of your creativity and joy, then find someone whose joy it is to clean and hire them to do it for you. Maintaining your beautiful surroundings is paramount when creating your relationship with your environment. What will you do for maintenance?

RELATIONSHIP WITH SELF-CREATED MISERY

"People have a hard time letting go of their suffering. Out of a fear of the unknown, they prefer suffering that is familiar." – Thich Nhat Hanh

One of the main tasks of becoming free is the understanding that you create your own misery. There are parts of yourself that you may try to deny, regret, or change: your DNA, your emotions, your past, anxiety about the future, self-created pain, and the opinions of others. Let's look at each area separately.

YOUR PARENTS AND THEIR REPRESENTATIONS IN THE WORLD

In my work with people, I have often heard women say their mother is their best friend. This has always been curious to me. While I love my mother, I would not classify her my friend, let alone my best friend. My mother has many wonderful qualities but, for most of my life, I have focused on the things "she should want to change." While I was focused on changing her, she was working hard to change me! Much of our relationship was misunderstanding one another and attempting to change each other.

The irony of this really hit me when I realized I was criticizing and complaining to my mother for her criticism and complaints about others. *What?* Yes, I was totally criticizing her while attempting to help her understand how bad criticizing and complaining are. This may seem like a no-brainer to you, but believe me, this realization eluded me for years.

Once I recognized it, you might think that would be the end of it, but recognition is just the beginning. There are new habits to create and practice. Today, whenever I think of my mother or interact with her, I do so with compassion. I look for understanding, and when I can't find it, I talk to others who might help me understand her more compassionately. It is easy to have compassion for a person when that is your goal. You keep looking until you find something you can empathize with, like, or understand.

Margaret Wheatley says, "It's hard to hate someone whose story you know." When I am having difficulty liking someone or finding compassion, I figure I need to get to know the person better.

I had a client who was the oldest child in a family with two younger brothers. Though all the children lived in the same house with the same father, each child had a very different relationship with him. She had the easiest relationship with her father. She was most like him and better able to understand the things he did, though she didn't always agree and had, at times, been embarrassed by the choices he made. The middle child was frequently disappointed in his father. He placed his father on the hero pedestal and saw him as perfect, which was fine as long as his father behaved perfectly, but that wasn't always possible. The youngest considered his father "no good" and spent all his energy and effort avoiding him. This seemed to help him cope with his father's unpredictable behavior, but his sister was concerned how her youngest brother will respond when their father dies. Will her brother forever regret not getting to know him better?

My client, who had the more neutral relationship, seemed to be the most emotionally healthy around that issue. When you deify or denigrate one of your parents, you are setting yourself up for disappointment or disconnection, neither of which serves you. Reaching a healthy place with your parents tends to occur after realizing they are regular people; there are things they do well and things they could do better. They are not perfect, nor are they villains. Being able to see your parents as human is a sure sign of maturity, emotional wellbeing, and freedom.

It is important for you to see your parents as they are, not as you might wish them to be. When you were little and still believed in the tooth fairy, your parents were your world and it was easy to place them on pedestals. Since they're your first teachers of morality, they appear to be perfect. It's typical to vilify your parents as a teenager. They become your jailers, keeping you from the important things you want to experience. As an adult, your task is to form a relationship with your parents based on who they actually are—fallible human beings, just like the rest of us.

Your parents have great qualities and some that are not-so-great. They have strengths and weaknesses. They have done wonderful, amazing things and they have made mistakes. They are not perfect, nor are they villains. The people who raised you did the best they were able to do, at the time, based on the information available to them. Can you forgive them for the mistakes they made and revel in the positive? Can you see their strengths as well as their shortcomings? Can you form a relationship with them based on your mutual humanity?

When you do, you will be free from childish thoughts of parental perfection. You will be able to accept your parents as they are. You will define the relationship you want to have with them without the guilt, anxiety, and obligation.

My client came to see me because her relationship with her father was strained. He had experienced a "mid-life crisis" and had started drinking and dating women younger than my client. She was frequently embarrassed by his behavior and wasn't sure she could even maintain a relationship with him. After considering the standard of behavior she was holding him to and exploring the possible needs her father was attempting to meet, she was able to feel compassion for him. She stopped needing him to be perfect for her, forgave him, and developed an adult relationship with him based on mutual respect.

If your parents are no longer living, you can still work to forgive them and let go of any regrets or resentment you may have. It might be helpful to write them a letter of what you'd like to say, and on an appropriate occasion, burn your letter and envision the energy of your words reaching a place your parents may hear them.

FREEDOM FROM YOUR EMOTIONS

Have you ever felt plagued by your emotions? When experiencing any painful emotion, it can seem to take on a life of its own and define you. Emotions are a very real part of the human experience, but you must learn to use them to your advantage instead of your detriment.

If you believe you are a victim to your emotions, it is now time to change that. If you believe in the biomedical disease model of mental illness perpetuated by psychiatry and pharmaceutical companies, then you have been told a lot of untruths. There is absolutely no conclusive evidence to support the "chemical imbalance" theory. If you don't believe that, I invite you to ask psychiatrists or pharmacists to show you the research that supports that theory. You will be surprised to find there isn't any.

If your emotions aren't a chemical imbalance, what are they? Chemicals are certainly part of it. A person experiencing love releases endorphins that feel really great. Someone who is scared is producing cortisol and adrenaline that can lead to fight, flight, or freeze behaviors. Emotions and chemicals are connected but, according to Choice Theory psychology, the chemicals are not causative.

Emotions are designed to help you recognize when something is "wrong" with your life. For example, you experience uncomfortable and painful emotions when you are not getting something you want. Painful emotions are meant to be your signal to either do or think something different, something that will lead to more desirable emotions. It is the actions and thoughts that are causative for the emotion, and the physiology your body produces.

When your world isn't the way you want it to be, you experience painful emotions, and other people respond in ways that sometimes meet your needs. Maybe they give you attention, assistance, space, a pass on your responsibilities—your emotion has a goal, whether you're aware of that goal `or not. When that goal is met, your subconscious learns to associate the emotion with the satisfaction of your need, making it more likely you will use it again. If you want to be free from your emotions, you need to understand what they are, what their purpose is, and what you are going to do about it. Take control of your emotions so they stop working against you and start working for you.

FREEDOM FROM THE PAST

"In order to love who you are, you cannot hate the experiences that have shaped you." – Andrea Dykstra

Are you haunted by past decisions or a memory of being wronged? Part of loving your Self is recognizing the past as a page in your life's story that has already been written. You cannot go back and edit what has been permanently recorded in the *Book of Life*. When I began learning the principles of Choice Theory, I was surprised by Dr. Glasser's lack of focus on history. After all, Freud, the father of modern psychiatry, taught his followers to discuss history at great length. There are still some who believe that, in order to move forward, it is necessary to understand, resolve, and put the past to rest. I do not believe that. Dr. William Glasser taught, "What happened in the past that was painful has a great deal to do with what we are today, but revisiting this painful past can contribute little or nothing to what we need to do now."

So as you come to peace with and free yourself from the past, there are only two steps to take, and an optional third, if you happen to be an overachiever:

1. **Honor your past.** It has shaped you into who you are today. If bad things happened to you that were out of your control, don't try to ignore or deny their existence, but also don't spend unnecessary

time there. You have no power over your past; there is only power in this moment.

2. If you or those close to you did something you regret or are angry about, **let it go.** Remind yourself of this principle of Choice Theory: everyone is doing their very best with the information available to them to get what they want at any given point in time. If they knew a better way, they would have done it. Forgive and move on. I love the quote that is not attributed to anyone specific, "Holding a grudge is like drinking poison and expecting the other person to die." Stop poisoning yourself. Don't allow that painful past to hold you hostage.

3. If you really want to feel good about your past, you can **start looking for the GLO** (Gift, Lesson, or Opportunity) in any painful experience. It's relatively easy to find the GLO with hindsight, but the real value comes from finding it in the moment. Since we are talking about the past here, can you look at what happened (whether someone hurt you or you made a mistake) and find a way you were helped by it? Did it change you in some way? Did it provide you with a skill or characteristic you didn't have before? Was there a lesson you learned? Perhaps you learned never to do *that* again! Is there an opportunity there you can capitalize on? The opportunity is typically a way for you to help others who are going through similar experiences. This step is optional, but I find that as horrible as the past might have been, there is an equal value of positivity around that same set of circumstances. You must first believe it is there and then be willing to explore until you find it. When you are able to achieve an equal positive/negative balance, it doesn't negate the pain but neutralizes it, allowing you to no longer be immobilized by the past event(s).

FREEDOM FROM ANXIETY ABOUT THE FUTURE

If you are a person who looks to the future with optimism, you won't need to read this section. If you are someone who thinks of the future with trepidation and anxiety, please continue reading. Worry is not only a huge waste of precious time, but it is also nonproductive and potentially harmful, both mentally and physically.

Are your concerns about the future keeping you from enjoying the present? I recently spoke with a woman who was worrying about her husband starting the new year on a very restrictive diet. She was sharing her concerns of how difficult it was going to be, not only for her husband but also for her, since she was experiencing a self-imposed need to come up with tasty recipes despite all the restrictions. Before even altering his diet, she was already worrying about the weight her already thin husband could lose. She was worried he would just stop eating all together and give up trying. The only part of her worries she could control were the recipes she needed to make. Nothing else was within her control, nor was it even a foregone conclusion. She was worrying about things that may never happen.

It is said that 90% of your worries are things that never happen, and the other 10% you couldn't have done anything about anyway, so why worry? From a Choice Theory perspective, all behavior is purposeful, which makes worry even more puzzling. If you look at what people are attempting to accomplish by worrying, it seems they want others to know how much they care. Worrying can prepare you to excuse failure. It's possible, somewhere in the subconscious, people actually believe that worrying will prevent the dreaded event from happening; every time they worry and nothing happens, that belief gets reinforced. If every time you are on a plane you worry about crashing and nothing happens, then you may actually come to believe that your worry is keeping the plane in the air! Of course, your conscious mind knows that's nonsense, but it still may be what's fueling your worry.

Would you like to free yourself from the grip of anxiety about the future? You need to develop a new inner dialogue.

Currently, there's a voice in your head telling you to worry about all kinds of things. Can you hear it? Does it shout or whisper?

There is a three-step process for putting that voice in its place:

1. Ask yourself if there is anything you can do to prepare for the worst case scenario of your biggest concern. If you are worried about a fire in the night, practice what you would do if that actually occurred. If you are concerned about bad storms, pack a go bag and imagine possible scenarios in your head until you have a reasonable action plan. Spend time in preparation for what you fear, but once you are adequately prepared, then let go of your anxiety. If there is nothing you can do, then move on to the next step.

2. Do not decide to battle with that dysfunctional, lying voice. That will give it too much power. That voice is just your subconscious talking to you about things that don't seem safe. Tune in and acknowledge its message, then respond with your empowering monologue. You might say something like, "I hear you little voice. Thank you for sharing, but you are mistaken! You are attempting to take my energy away to focus on things that haven't even happened yet. I don't want to waste my precious moments worrying about whatever you are talking about. If and when something happens, I'll deal with it then."

3. Distraction is another great technique for combating anxiety. What can you do differently that will take your mind away from worrying? Doing something that requires brain power will be beneficial in this scenario. Read something, do a puzzle, or have a conversation with a friend. Choose anything that will align you with the present moment rather than wasting the moment worrying about something that will likely never

happen.

Relax and enjoy this moment. Have you ever noticed there is really nothing wrong right now, right this minute? Eckhart Tolle says, "The only place where you can or need to be free is this moment." Everything is perfect if you just take the time to notice. And when it isn't, do what you can to fix it. If it's something you can't change, figure out how you will adjust yourself.

FREEDOM FROM SELF-CREATED PAIN

"It is almost impossible for anyone, even the most ineffective among us, to continue to choose misery after becoming aware that it is a choice."

– William Glasser

Too much of our pain is self-created. This is one of the more difficult parts of Choice Theory to understand, because it requires you to take responsibility for the suffering you are choosing. No one wants to believe they are choosing or creating their own misery; it's much easier to reject the information. However, once you understand and begin to apply it, you gain freedom from your pain, and that is one giant step forward toward *Choosing Me Now*.

Choice Theory states that all behavior is purposeful and most of that behavior is chosen. In Choice Theory, behavior consists of four inseparable components—the actions you take, the thoughts you think, the emotions you experience, and the internal workings of your body, i.e. blood pressure, digestion, heart rate, breathing, etc. You do not have the ability to directly change your emotions or your body's processes but, if you want those things to change, you can directly change or control your thoughts and your actions. It cannot be argued that uninvited thoughts can intrude upon your consciousness. However, when you experience a thought you do not want to entertain, you possess the ability to direct your mind elsewhere.

Let's say you're feeling devastated after someone you love ended your relationship. As long as you entertain the thoughts about the other person, you will continue to feel devastated.

Trying to determine what is "wrong" with you that caused your loved one to let you go is a battle with no end. Should you decide you no longer want to feel devastated, you will need to make changes to what you are doing and what you are thinking.

It may sound like I am saying it's easy. It's not easy, but neither was riding a bicycle before you learned how. Anything you found difficult to learn at first may now be second nature to you, like riding a bike. The same is true about being able to indirectly change your feelings and body processes through a conscious and deliberate decision to act and think differently.

Why would people choose misery? First of all, most people do not know it is a choice. It certainly doesn't *feel* like a choice, but like something that just overtakes you, masquerading as something beyond your control. It's a cruel trick that keeps you locked in your pain and misery for an indeterminate amount of time.

Why would you, or anyone else, stay stuck in misery? Often, it's the only way you know to move closer to what you want. Choosing misery can result in the following:

1. **Retention**: It's the only way to keep someone or something you've lost active in your mind. It is no longer part of your daily existence, so you continue to ruminate about the loss to keep it active in your mind.
2. **Attention**: It gets you the attention you desperately want.
3. **Help**: It can get you assistance from others when you're unable or unwilling to ask for help directly.
4. **Control**: It can control others by causing them to feel guilty or sorry for you, so they become more willing to do what you want.
5. **Importance**: Misery, albeit subconsciously, shows others how important the loss was to you. If you are too resilient, bouncing back too quickly, you may be judged as someone who really didn't care about the loss, whatever it was.
6. **Freedom**: It can help free you from certain

responsibilities or obligations. When you are miserable, people don't always expect you to go to work, clean the house, pay your bills, or take care of your children.

7. **Space**: It can slow life down for you, giving you the time and space you need to figure out your next step.

8. **Connection**: It can bond you to others who are feeling the same way, creating a shared experience.

9. **Safety**: In severe cases, sometimes misery takes the form of depression to keep you safe. It can immobilize you, preventing you from engaging in self-harm or the harm of others. People who provide crisis intervention services know that the most critical time to watch suicidal individuals is when their depression starts to lift. It is theorized that people are more likely to suicide at that time because they have more energy and clarity of thought to follow through on their desire to end their life. So severe depression can keep you safe.

10. **Habit**: Sometimes your misery isn't working for you at all. It may have worked in the beginning, but you can no longer find any benefit to it. It has become a habit because you haven't yet developed a new behavior that works better. When you develop behaviors that work, they tend to become habitual, and you will continue to use them long after they have served their usefulness.

Now that you understand how pain and misery can serve you, are you able to identify the benefit you receive from yours? This question is not posed for you to judge or punish yourself. Remember, most of this happens at a subconscious level, beyond your conscious awareness. Not only that, but it also represents the best you knew to do with the information available to you at that point in time.

Now you have new information, and you need to decide

if it fits for you. You may identify how misery is benefiting you and stick to it, deciding that you can't think of anything that will work better. More often, as Dr. Glasser's quote states, once you become aware you are choosing your misery, it will be difficult for you to maintain it.

After recognizing the way your self-inflicted misery is benefiting you, it's likely you will want to do something different. Depending on the type of person you are, in combination with the context for the behavior, it'll be easier to do one or the other: act your way into a new behavior, or think your way into a new behavior. I'm typically a "think your way" kind of person, but you may find it easier to "act your way" into a new behavior. It doesn't matter which path you take as both will create a new behavior, creating new emotions and body processes.

The question becomes, "What am I going to do or think differently that will lead me to the place I want to be?" Just as misery is a choice, so is the choice you make to move away from your pain. I will provide some possible options, but they are only suggestions. You need to choose what seems like the best option for you.

1. **Retention**: (*Acting*) Create a physical way of commemorating the person—a scholarship fund, a plaque, a piece of jewelry with some of their ashes, a private personal space to meditate and remember that person. (*Thinking*) Find ways to experience that person's essence still with you— in your memories, your dreams, your heart or spiritually. Think the person may be "in a better place," or that he or she is doing what is "right" for him or her. If it's a thing that was lost, see it as an opportunity opening for something even better, and watch for signs of what's positive to come.

2. **Attention**: (*Acting*) Specifically ask for what you want or find another person willing to give you the attention you crave. (*Thinking*) Contemplate better ways to gain attention with less negative effects on you.

3. **Help**: (*Acting*) Ask directly for the help you need, hire someone to do it, or decide you can and will do it yourself. (*Thinking*) Either "I am capable of doing this myself" or "There is no shame admitting I need help. No one, not even me, can do everything without help."

4. **Control**: (*Acting*) Asking directly for what you want from others, and move on if you can't get it. Do not resort to external control; instead, find a person willing to do what you want or figure out how to do it on your own. (*Thinking*) "I do not have the right to guilt anyone into doing things my way. I will find another way to get what I want, decide it's no longer important to me, or find something else even more important."

5. **Importance**: (*Acting*) Again, find a way to memorialize the person in a public way. (*Thinking*) "I know how important this person was to me. It doesn't matter what others think," and possibly, "The person I lost would not want me moping around. S/he would want me to be living my life."

6. **Freedom**: (*Acting*) Start doing the things you are responsible for, whether or not you want to. Jumping in and taking care of things will be rewarding enough to provide the impetus you need to continue moving forward. (*Thinking*) "I am ready to resume my responsibilities. I know it won't be easy but it is important that I take of myself and what is mine."

7. **Space**: (*Action*) Make a conscious decision to take the time you need; plan some time alone to strategize. (*Thinking*) "I have every right to take the time I need to figure out what I want to do."

8. **Connection**: (*Acting*) Use positive experiences and characteristics to connect with people. For the ones going through similar difficulties, find ways to connect by sharing your positive spin

on things. (*Thinking*) Ask yourself, "Do I really want to connect on such a negative plane?" Think about positive ways this tragedy may help you and others in the long run. Think about other things you may have in common with the people you want to connect with.

9. **Safety:** (*Acting*) If you recognize you are depressing for safety, it may be the best choice available to you right now. Create a safety plan. Make a list of supportive people you can reach out to when feeling desperate. (*Thinking*) Remember that depressing may be keeping you safe and accept it. Remind yourself that sometimes we need to jack up the pain in order to make changes on the other side of it.

10. **Habit:** (*Acting*) To act yourself out of a habit, you must recognize when you're engaging in the habit and consciously change your behavior. You might choose calling a friend, journaling, or listening to music. Any change will do. (*Thinking*) Remembering, "Here I go again. This is just a habit kicking in. I'm grateful I'm noticing it. This will help me do something different next time."

FREEDOM FROM THE OPINIONS AND EXPECTATIONS OF OTHERS

So often the opinions and expectations of others—sometimes well-meaning, sometimes more sinister—hold us hostage, preventing us from creating the freedom we desire. The things we want to do are obstructed by the thought of what others will think or remembering what they want from us. People may try to convince you that what you are doing isn't a good idea, and they will also have ideas of what you *should* be doing. Their expectations for you and your life will not always align with what you want for your life. I can think of two instances in my own life where this came into play.

When I was a teenager, I dreamed of being a concert

pianist. I had natural talent and had been taking lessons since I was six. I wanted to attend Julliard, as all aspiring pianists did, when a casual comment made by my mother stopped me dead in my tracks. She told me, "You don't want to do that. You would never be able to have a family with that kind of travel schedule." And I believed her. With the benefit of hindsight, I think that was for the best. I really was meant to be a helping a professional, but even if I had been destined to be a pianist, my mother's words might have put me on a different path.

Back when I was planning to leave my job, move to Chicago, and start my own business, my best friend at the time asked me, "Why would you want to do that? When you work for someone else, you only have one boss. When you have your own business, every client you have is a boss!" I believe she was genuinely trying to help me, but the fact that she expected we would always be friends living in the same area may have been an ulterior motive. I'm thankful I didn't follow that advice and stayed on my true path, listening only to my inner voice that has helped me create the ideal life for myself.

When you don't pursue what you want most in fear of what people will say, you are letting the opinions and expectations of others stop you. It's normal to want the voice of popular opinion on your side, but there are many opinions out there—some you agree with, others you don't. You may be rejected by some for the actions you take, but others who approve of your actions will step in to fill the void.

I once worked with an African American male who was in love with a Caucasian female. By his own admission, it was the best relationship he had ever had. The relationship itself was supporting, encouraging, and loving beyond anything he had experienced prior; the stress he experienced came from the opinions and expectations of others. Some of his female friends judged him as a traitor, telling him he should stick to his own race and asking if he had stopped appreciating women of color. He had not, but he still wanted to continue his relationship with this white woman. Unfortunately, the path of public opinion overwhelmed his desire for the woman he loved, and he ended their relationship, creating a different type of misery.

When it comes to making decisions for *your* life, you are the one and only best person to make them. You are the one who must live with the consequences. No one else is able to determine what is best for you because they are *not* you! There is not one person in your life who has the exact same values, beliefs, and experiences as you do; the only real advice someone could give you is what he or she might do in a similar situation. No one knows what it would be like to be you in *your* situation.

You may believe you cannot go on without the approval of your family or friends. However, when people leave you because of the choices you make, it is typically their loss, not yours. Other people who support you and your right to live the life you choose will fill the void left by those who judged and criticized you. *Choosing Me Now* is about taking the path you believe is best regardless of what others say. Just because someone wants you to do something doesn't mean you are obligated to. Thank them for their concern and follow your inner voice. If it doesn't work out, you are the only one who must live with the consequences; when it does, you are the one to reap the vast rewards! What choices have you made because of other people's opinions and expectations despite wanting to choose something else? Is it time to reconsider your choices?

When you have finally freed yourself from the opinions and expectations of others, you will work at making sure your needs for Safety & Security, Significance, Freedom, Joy, and Connection are met.

RELATIONSHIP WITH YOUR ABILITY TO BE YOURSELF

"The artist is no other than he who unlearns what he has learned, in order to know himself." – E.E. Cummings

If this is a difficult area for you, it usually stems from not knowing who you are, letting your concerns about what others think hold your true Self back, or waiting for a life event to happen that will allow you to truly start living. When you have a healthy relationship with your Self, you continuously explore and create improved aspects of yourself. While you care about others and listen to their opinions, if those opinions don't fit your world view, you say thank you and continue doing what makes you happy, as long as it doesn't prevent others from meeting their needs.

KNOWING YOURSELF

If you don't know who you are, it may be because you have been subjected to a controlling, stifling environment that allowed you no personal freedom. Existing in an environment where being your Self has severe consequences, you learn fear and compliance as a way of self-preservation. In my job as a foster care worker, I encountered children raised in this type of environment. As I got to know them, I realized all they knew about themselves was how to please and avoid their abuser. Adults can also end up in this type of environment through criminal activity, abusive marriages, and organized groups that strictly control its members.

When you are trying to have a loving relationship with yourself and have come from this type of environment, either as a child or adult, you have some work to do. You have been programmed to accept things you wouldn't have chosen on your own. When this happens systematically over time, then you likely believe things to be true that are, in fact, lies told to control you.

Here are the steps to recover from that programming:

1. Realize that by virtue of the fact that you are alive, you deserve to be free.
2. Make your safety your number one priority.
   a. If you are free of the oppressive environment, get to a place where you feel safe.
   b. If you are still in the environment and can safely leave, then do so.
   c. If you are in the oppressive environment and can't safely leave, then create a safe

space in your mind to have your free thoughts, even if your actions are being controlled by others.

3. When you are safe, begin to ask yourself the question, "What would I want if I had no one telling me what I'm *supposed* to want?"

4. If you hear a contradicting voice in your head, ask your Self, "Is that true? Is that *really* true, or is it a lie I've been tricked or coerced into believing?" Ask your Self, "What would I want if I knew my beliefs were lies I was taught by someone wanting to control me?"

5. Remind your Self that you are safe and there will be no further consequences. You are out of the environment that had a hold on you.

6. If you truly don't know what you want, explore new situations and keep asking your Self, "Does this feel good to me? Does it fit with the person I want to be?" Should you continue to hear that critical, oppressive voice, repeat steps four through six.

If you really don't know who you are but weren't exposed to a controlling environment, then you are likely a people pleaser. People pleasers are so busy trying to anticipate and fulfill the needs of the people around them that they have no time to discover their true desires. This is particularly true for people who have a high need for Connection; their need for relationships supersedes their want of anything that may put that relationship at risk. This how I define codependency.

Many people define codependency as what occurs when one person in a relationship consistently prioritizes their partner's needs over their own, but I don't think it is that simple. You can be a person who chooses to prioritize what someone else wants, and doing so meets your Connection need; it meets that need because it feels good to do something for someone else. If you are the one in your relationship with a high Connection need, you are more likely to prioritize your relationship and do things for the other person. If you find that satisfying, then it is not dysfunctional. If you see your Self as a helpful, selfless person, then helping others matches that picture. It feels great when your actions align with your beliefs about your Self. To an outside observer, it might look like you are sacrificing yourself for someone else, but in reality, you know you are doing exactly what makes *you* happy. This is healthy.

On the other hand, when you do things for others you don't want to do, you may be codependent. In the first scenario, there would be no insecurity, fear, or resentment. In this scenario, these are exactly the emotions you experience. If you are codependent and terrified of losing the relationship, you sacrifice yourself and what you want in favor of pleasing someone else. Doing this habitually results in you having no idea what you really want. You're too involved in constantly taking the temperature of the relationship, willing to do whatever it takes to maintain a homeostasis.

If this is your situation, it is critical that you begin to have a loving relationship with yourself, which probably sounds like a "crazy" or "stupid" idea to you. You may not even imagine how a relationship with yourself could be satisfying. The exciting and delightful thing about loving your Self is that, when you invest in that relationship, the quality of the people you attract exponentially increases. If it's difficult to imagine the satisfaction of a relationship with yourself, how do you figure anyone else will find it satisfying?

I once worked with a codependent woman who said, "My husband is the sun. I am the moon. My life revolves around him." Because she was scared he would leave her, she constantly monitored his mood and desires so she could adjust and attempt to provide whatever he wanted. Her husband said he was tired of living with a person who lacked substance. The couple got divorced, making the very thing she was trying to prevent a reality.

Being free to be your Self is essential in loving yourself. If this still isn't clear, consider this parable my friend and public speaker, Marcus Gentry, shares with his audiences. Imagine that when we are born, we are issued an all access ticket to the Amusement Park of Life. The front of the ticket displays the date and time of your birth, and on the back, in invisible ink, is your expiration date. You don't know when it is, but you know you have one. With this ticket, you're given the ability and permission to do whatever you want in the park. You can ride the roller coaster a million times over. You can ride the bumper cars, the Ferris wheel, and the carousel as many times as you want. You can hop over to the water park for some water rides. You can walk up and down the midway, playing the games and eating carnival food. You can even sit on the bench, watching everyone else use their tickets. But the one thing you cannot do is tell others how they should use their tickets. You have your own ticket to use—you cannot use other people's tickets. It's their ticket, not yours!

Conversely, do not relinquish your ticket to someone else—you only get one. There is no one in the park worth forfeiting your ticket to. So take it and use it however you like, but do not allow others to rob you of your choices and your life.

There is no rule that will prevent you from giving your ticket away. You *can* surrender your ticket to someone else, but in doing so, you ensure a life of not knowing or liking who you are. You need to explore the park, decide what you like, and do what brings you joy. Anyone who tries to take your ticket or tells you how to use it does not have your best interests in mind. They are trying to control you, rob you of your free will, and make your choices for you. Being free to be you is essential in having a healthy relationship with your Self.

CONCERN ABOUT OTHERS

The fear of loss, disapproval, or judgment from others can keep you from feeling free to be your Self. This makes you believe that sacrificing your own well-being is the only way to help someone else be happy. This is a trap; don't fall for it.

You may believe exercising your right to be your Self is selfish, particularly if it "hurts" other people. Remember that people, either consciously or subconsciously, use their pain to control others; don't fall prey to this trap. Make the decision to follow your own path, to be responsible for your own happiness, and to realize following your passion is not a selfish act—it's actually the opposite. When you don't follow your inner passion, you rob the world of something good, possibly even great, to appease people in your life who would choose feeling hurt by your choices over being supportive.

Sometimes being your Self can cause pain for others, so it may be necessary to leave some people behind. When you follow your passion, those close to you who aren't following theirs may become envious or feel slighted in some way. Being your Self can be a lonely journey in the beginning as old associations fall away before new ones are in place—don't lose heart! The closer you come to being your Self, you will attract the supportive and encouraging people that are meant to be in your life.

As I improved my life, the quality of my friends, associates, and even clients matched with what I wanted. Yes, I lost some people along the way, but I no longer miss them. As they work towards becoming who they are supposed to be, there is a place for them in my life. Until then, we will spend less time together, and that is an acceptable trade off to me.

There will always be people in your life that do not want you to change, people invested in keeping you exactly as you are. It suits them and their plans for their own life. However, you do not have to sign on as a coconspirator in their plan. Make the moves your heart instructs you to make, and those who are meant to be a part of that journey will be there for you. The others will fall by the wayside so you can be free to be you.

LIFE EVENTS

Perhaps you are waiting for life events before feeling free enough to be your Self. *I'll be able to do what I want when I retire, when my parents die, when the kids are grown, once I get my degree, when my bank account reaches a certain amount...* You may have legitimate reasons for waiting, but I would ask you, "What's something you can do while you are waiting that will pave the way for you when you are ready?" There is never a reason to do nothing. If you are not on the path you know is there for you, there is always something you can do to move in its direction.

Being as free as you need to be is critical in the process of creating a healthy relationship with your Self. Being kept from experiencing the Freedom you need will cause resentment towards the people or situations holding you back. When you see yourself being resentful in the world, you will not like the person you see. You may end up resenting yourself for allowing your freedom to be compromised.

To summarize, if you want more Freedom for yourself, then be more free. Freedom isn't something that comes from outside of you. You were born with the drive to be free, to make your own way, and to thwart restrictions. The biggest struggle toward Freedom happens inside your own head where you allow yourself to be imprisoned. If you want more Freedom in your life, you must recognize you hold the key to that prison and can let your Self out any time you choose. You simply need to remember, and *be* free.

What doesn't work:

1. Living without a space you love.
2. Putting your parents on a pedestal.
3. Holding grudges.
4. Believing you are a victim of your emotions.
5. Trusting someone else's opinion more than your own.
6. Prioritizing someone else's needs above your own even when that's not what you want to do.

What does:

1. Creating an environment that nurtures you.
2. Viewing your parents as human—people with positive qualities capable of making mistakes.
3. Forgiving those you perceive have wronged you.
4. Understanding emotions as an attempt to get something you want and changing your actions and thoughts to create the emotions you want to experience.
5. Tuning into your own voice and following its advice.
6. Learning your own preferences and doing what brings you joy.

JOY

"Joy collected over time fuels resilience." – Brené Brown

*A*re you someone who prioritizes Joy over almost anything else? Do you tend to avoid anything you perceive is without joy? Do you have a great sense of humor and like to laugh? Is making others laugh important to you? Do you seek learning opportunities for the joy of discovery? Do you prioritize relaxation? In this chapter, you'll determine how much Joy you need in your life. Perhaps you won't do anything without finding the joy in it, or maybe joy is just a byproduct of the things you do to fulfill your other needs.

Play, relaxation, and learning all satisfy the basic human need for Joy, though you may play more than you relax, relax more than you learn, or do all at once!

It is important to understand the level of Joy that's necessary in your life. Having enough will result in contentment, and not having enough will cause boredom, apathy, and, of course, sadness. With depleted levels of Joy, you will feel driven to satisfy this need.

You may make a conscious decision to forego joy during a challenging period in your life. Perhaps you put joy on the back burner to focus on completing a project, paying off bills, or going to school. It won't be long before you will need to answer the call to experience Joy in your life.

Even with a low need for Joy, it will take priority when it isn't being met, especially in serious situations that offer no opportunities for joy. If you are anywhere where joy is difficult to experience—a war zone, prison, a hospital cancer ward, for example—the need for Joy will be so strong, you may fill the void with gallows humor. The need for Joy hasn't actually become stronger, it's moved to the center of your attention because you're having greater difficulty meeting it.

Having too much Joy may seem harmless, but it can become problematic when it prevents you from meeting your other needs. An excess of Joy may prevent you from accomplishing your goals, connecting to your loved ones, or acknowledging a deeper problem. You can also choose Joy options that put your safety at risk: extreme sports, excessive drinking, or frivolous spending, for example.

When you need more Joy in your life, there are a multitude of options. It will help you to know what your preferred joyful experiences typically entail. Do you prefer more active types of joy, quiet relaxing joy, or the joy that comes from meaningful learning? Once you know that answer, you can tap into your Quality World for things that met this need in the past or think about new ways to create Joy in your life.

You can increase the options of play, relaxation, or learning for yourself. If you aren't making time for Joy, then work at creating the time. If you don't have things in your life you find enjoyable, then do some exploration to discover something new. Talk to and observe those close to you for some new ideas. What do your favorite fictional characters do for joy? What did you love as a child? You can organize a get together with people you enjoy, take a hike in the mountains, or sign up for a class you have been wanting to take. You may even create Joy by finding the humor in whatever humorless situation you may find yourself in. Ask yourself, "What can I do to increase the level of Joy in my life?"

It is important to have options for Joy that don't cost a lot of money, and also options you can do by yourself. There will be times you won't have much money or may be alone. When all else fails, use the power of your perception to turn anything you do into something enjoyable. As Jenny Lundak, basic Choice

Theory instructor, says, "When you find yourself in situations that don't involve a lot of Joy, you can still find ways to enjoy what you are doing." People who don't like to exercise can listen to audio books while working out to make it more enjoyable. When you have a horrible or disgusting mess to clean, you can focus on the ridiculousness of the task and laugh at yourself and the situation. You can even listen to music to give you an enjoyable distraction while you clean. Remember the song "A Spoonful of Sugar" in *Mary Poppins?* The song opens with the lyrics, "In every job that must be done there is an element of fun. You find the fun and, snap, the job's a game." Finding the humor in life is a tool that will always keep options for Joy at your fingertips. There were moments in my life that if I couldn't laugh, I'd cry! It involves shifting your perception to shape an unfavorable situation into an enjoyable one. Transform tedious, unpleasant tasks into something enjoyable and your whole experience changes. Find the humor, use your brain, change your thoughts, and create the Joy you need.

If you need more Joy, more Connection, Safety & Security, Significance, or Freedom will not satisfy you; Joy is what you need.

You may have some subconscious rules about Joy. Perhaps you reward yourself with enjoyment only after your work is done, or maybe you contain your happiness so others around you don't think you're bragging about your life. Examine these rules closely and determine if they prevent you from having a healthy relationship with your Self. You may feel there are certain settings where experiencing joy is wrong, such as a funeral, or one of the aforementioned "serious situations." I would say these are the times when creating Joy is most important. These rules get in the way of you experiencing Joy, but being joyful will attract other joyful people into your life. You may have some who become jealous to the point they stop spending time with you; though you may lose people, higher vibrational people will take their place.

Limiting beliefs may construct a false comfort zone for Joy in your life. If you think your level of Joy can't exceed that of those around you, you will curtail the level of happiness in your life. You may believe you don't deserve Joy in your life because of some shortcoming you perceive or others have pointed out to you. Staying in this self-imposed comfort zone will not serve you, particularly if Joy is one of your higher needs. Denying yourself Joy can lead to misery.

When I was teaching Choice Theory to an audience that had a preliminary understanding of it, several participants didn't think they had a need for Fun (that is what Dr. Glasser called this need) because they only thought fun involved the joking, active kind of fun. From that point on, I have always included relaxation and learning as integral parts of Joy. Which of these creates Joy for you?

The sections of this chapter are about your relationships with play, relaxation, and useful learning. When you have a positive relationship with play, you know how to have fun, often with others, and don't deny yourself those opportunities. When you have a positive relationship with relaxation, you understand how important rest is to your life and can find enjoyment in more quiet, maybe solitary activities. When you have a healthy relationship with relevant learning, you view yourself as a perpetual student, always seeking the Joy of discovery. Meeting the level of Joy you need in your life is part of the puzzle of creating a healthy relationship with your Self. What are the ways you have for creating Joy in your life?

RELATIONSHIP WITH PLAY

"Time flies whether you're having fun or not. The choice is yours."
– Unknown

*P*lay encompasses a plethora of activities; how you have fun is unique to you. Maybe you have fun being active: skiing, swimming, biking, traveling, hiking, bungee jumping, playing with pets, dancing, kayaking, horseback riding, and sporting activities. It's totally possible to relax and have fun too: art, crafts, cooking, spending time with friends and family, board or card games, reading, and writing. You name it, and it will be fun for someone! Having fun produces the chemicals oxytocin and serotonin in our bodies. You smile, laugh, and feel good doing it.

There are fortunate people who find enjoyment through their work. Confucius said, "Do something you love and you will never work a day in your life." I tried to engrain this into my children's heads.

I am fortunate because whenever I work with audiences, I consider that play and it brings me great Joy. I get to tell stories with my own brand of humor, creating learning opportunities for others.

Some of my colleagues include creativity within the need for Joy, though, for me, the ability to be creative fits best under the Freedom need. Fun can be a *result* of creativity, but for me, the ability to be creative fits best under the Freedom need. It's perfectly normal if you consider being creative part of Joy; the uniqueness from person to person regarding how needs are classified is one of the things that makes Choice Theory's Basic Needs so fascinating.

There are no limits to how children create play in their lives; they play with paper, pots and pans, and their food, and have a blast doing not much at all! A child does not need to be reminded to play; that is something every child knows how to do. As you have grown older and assumed more responsibilities, however, you may have forgotten the importance of play in your life.

It is likely adults may have sent you early childhood messages about not being able to play until your work was done. When you are five, there isn't a lot of work to do, so there is plenty of time for playing. When you are ten, school, homework, chores, and maybe some extracurricular activities leave less time for play. By the time you are a teenager, you typically add a part-time job into the mix and prioritize play on the weekends. Adulthood comes with a full-time job, housework, and bills to pay. On top of all of that, you may have pets or children to attend to. Time for play as an adult can become quite limited.

If you bought into the idea that play is for after your work is done, you may never get around to it. It's common to hear middle-aged adults lamenting they are waiting for retirement so they can finally play. This is a travesty! Play is an aspect of the Joy need that people need to meet every day, not just when their work is completed or they are retired.

You can find ways to play in everything you do, it can be as simple as engaging your sense of humor. I have a friend that always puts on seventies music while she does her housework, so she dances her way through her household chores. Even while working, people with a high need for Joy will find ways to laugh and play. This is healthy.

What kind of play do you like to engage in? When was the last time you did? Can you find a way to incorporate a little play into every day? Setting aside time to laugh, even when you don't feel like laughing, releases oxytocin and serotonin into your bloodstream. Research has shown that a fake laugh benefits you the same as a genuine laugh, so what are you waiting for? Get your laugh on right now!

You might balk at the idea of enjoying yourself, particularly if you're convinced that everything you like to do is expensive. Take some time to make a list of all the things you enjoy that cost under ten dollars. See if you can get to one hundred things!

In order to nurture your relationship with your Self, please be sure to create some active play in your life every day. If this type of fun is not for you, perhaps you prefer a more relaxing type of Joy.

RELATIONSHIP WITH RELAXATION

"Tension is who you think you should be. Relaxation is who you are."
– Chinese Proverb

*I*f you are someone who prefers relaxing for enjoyment, you might like taking walks in the woods, fishing, meditating, or reading on your porch swing. Taking some down time out of the craziness that is your life helps you prioritize your needs and take care of your Self.

This has not always been an easy area for me, but I have been improving since writing this book. Back when people were telling me to "take care of myself," I realized that they may have been telling me I needed to slow down and relax. With the research and writing of this book, I have discovered how important that is.

I was in a period of overwork in my life. Yes, I was social, but typically with people I had work connections with. I wasn't involved in a romantic relationship. I love my work; it was not a hardship, but I didn't do much else. It didn't feel like I was laboring, toiling, or exhausting myself. The work I do nurtures me—it meets my Safety & Security need by paying the bills; the Significance need by allowing me to make a difference in the lives of the people I speak with; the Freedom need by allowing me to travel, set my own schedule, create my own material; the Joy need because I enjoy the work and laugh often with my audiences; and the Connection need because I am always meeting and making new friends while visiting old ones. Why did I need to relax too?

I realized I was constantly multitasking. I thought I was having memory issues but, the truth of the matter is, I wasn't fully present with the people I was talking to, so memories of conversions were spotty. Even as I watched a movie, read a book, or did some other relaxing activity, I would want to simultaneously be doing something else. I might also play a Sudoku game, fold laundry, or answer emails.

Today, if I saw someone else behaving in this way, I might also ask, "What are you doing to take care of yourself?" It's not surprising that people were worried about my wellbeing. I decided that others worrying about my welfare was not what was going to help me move in a positive direction. I needed to take on that personal responsibility myself.

I was finally aware that relaxation is necessary, and I needed to implement it in my life. The question for me was, "What does it mean to fully relax?" I learned a simple technique that helps with mindfulness and actually develops an ability to go to sleep. It's called the 4-7-8 breathing technique (*https://goo.gl/7rLp5X*). Basically, you inhale through your nose to the count of four, hold your breath for the count of seven, and then exhale through your mouth to the count of eight. Repeat as many times as you like, but four times is typically what is needed to achieve deep relaxation. I began using it to fall asleep and, so far, it has never failed me.

Another quick breathing technique is to take deep breaths in through your nose and out through your mouth. Inhale deeply, exhale slowly—the end of the exhale marks the first count. Do the same for the second, repeating up to ten. Then work backwards to zero. This technique is called Twenty Breaths, and it is helpful when you need to achieve quick relaxation and focus.

There are a multitude of ways to find enjoyment through relaxation: yoga, meditation, saunas, hot tubs, sleep, bubble baths, and massages. Experiencing the arts, listening to music, seeing a good movie, or reading a good book are also great relaxation options.

Getting enough sleep is another result of having a healthy relationship with relaxation. You will stop prioritizing anything over your own health; you will begin to prioritize a good night's sleep over most everything else. In realizing how valuable you are, you will see how relaxation is required to keep up with the pace of being on your path of passion. Determine what works best for you, and make sure you get enough relaxation in your life.

RELATIONSHIP WITH LEARNING

"What we learn with pleasure we never forget." – Alfred Mercier

After years of memorizing math equations, scientific terms, and the names of dead generals, you may be sick of irrelevant, non-useful learning. This incomplete image of learning may have held you back from expanding your knowledge. It may be hard to believe, but there are opportunities for relevant, useful learning, and it's an integral part of the Joy need. Setting a goal to learn something new each day will keep you on the lookout for these opportunities that exist all around you.

There is wisdom to extract from every new person and situation you encounter, especially in areas where you believe you made a mistake—there's always a lesson to uncover if you're willing to look for it.

You will stop learning from the people and situations in your path when you believe you know all there is to know. When you don't think people who are less successful than you have things to teach you, you are in dangerous territory. When you stop looking for the lessons in everyday life, you begin to blame things outside yourself for the pain you experience instead of learning lessons you need to know for your life's journey.

Once I was straightening my office, took a blind step, and lost my balance. I tried to grasp onto my chair to get back on my feet, but it fell on me instead, pinning me against the arm of my futon which dug into my left side. A few interesting contortions later, I was on my feet and remember thinking, *You're going to have some bruise tomorrow!* Tomorrow came, I had the bruise I expected, but also some unexpected pain on my right side. The next day, it was excruciatingly painful to sit down, so I spent more time on my feet, until shooting pains down my right leg caused my knee to give out. I fell three times, and by then I was pretty scared. A friend insisted on taking me to urgent care, where they took one look at me and sent me to the ER for an MRI. They gave me a knee brace and enough pain medicine to last until my appointment with an orthopedic back surgeon. The pain was worse than when I broke both of my ankles, and the narcotic pain medicine hardly helped.

I ran out of medicine, and the surgeon couldn't prescribe anything until he saw me. My general practitioner was out of town, and since I hadn't seen her in over a year, no one in her office could help me. The ER could prescribe me more pain medicine, but I would have had to pay for a second visit which was something I didn't want to do. So for five days, I was in some serious pain. I couldn't eat, sleep, or concentrate on anything.

A week before my fall, I was listening to CDs about the Law of Attraction. I knew if I stayed focused on how much pain I was in, I would only attract more pain into my life—definitely not what I wanted to do. But how does one stop focusing on pain when that is all that is being experienced? I remembered a book by Gay Hendricks that talked about visualizing away the pain. I thought it was a bit hokey, but I was desperate. I sat in my chair, closed my eyes, and started meditative deep breathing. After about five minutes, I felt my cramped muscles begin to relax and was able to pinpoint two sources of pain, my lower right back and my right hip joint. I sent love and light to those places and imagined wrapping the pain in cotton so it wouldn't hurt anymore. It took an exceptional amount of energy to maintain focus but as long as I stayed focused, I didn't feel the pain. What Gay Hendricks had written about actually worked for me!

When I was able to experience some time without pain, I was also able to contemplate what possible gifts, lessons, or opportunities (GLO) came from this accident. Through meditation, I realized the pain from this, what should have been, a minuscule accident could be my future if I continued on a path of minimal exercise. My older years may be filled with pain, inactivity, and sleepless nights.

On the Wayne Dyer CDs I had been listening to, I learned that bad things happen to provide us with contrast. We need to experience what we *don't* want in order to understand what we *do* want. This accident made that clear: I was being shown what I didn't want, providing me with incentive to make a change. I would no longer say I don't want to exercise—I *do* want to exercise so I will have freedom of movement in my older years! I also met and established a regular relationship with an incredible massage therapist. She comes to my home to work on me, is amazingly generous with her time, and is the most skilled therapist I've ever met. I would never have met her if not for this accident. There is always GLO as long as you are willing to seek it.

You may be wondering how this anecdote connects to this section: it was my desire for continuous learning that provided me with the tools I used to get through that challenging time. Several years ago, I had read that book by Gay Hendricks, and I visualized my pain away. Just the week prior, I had been listening to the CDs with Abraham and Wayne Dyer, and I realized I was harming myself by focusing on the pain. What do you do to expand your base of knowledge?

If you want more Joy in your life, then be more playful, relaxed, and open to learning. Joy isn't something you go out and get, but something you create and bring with you in all that you do. It's the attitude you create for your life; it's the focus you choose to have. You may find Joy externally, but it will be fleeting. The permanent, never-fail-you type of joy is always with you. Tap into your endless supply, laugh, and be happy. The ability to enjoy, whether it be through play, relaxation, or relevant learning, already exists inside you. You simply need to remember and *be* playful, relaxed, and open to learning.

What doesn't work:

1. Waiting until your work is done to play.
2. Never fully relaxing, always multitasking.
3. Constantly pushing yourself to be productive.
4. Believing you know all there is to know.

What does:

1. Playing somehow every day.
2. Finding the Joy in everything you do.
3. Making sure you get enough rest and relaxation.
4. Learning from all people and every situation.
5. Being open to learning from painful experiences.
6. Learning your own preferences and doing what brings you Joy.

CONNECTION

"Human knowledge is never contained in one person. It grows from the relationships we create between each other and the world, and still it is never complete." – Paul Kalanithi

I believe the need for Connection, even if it isn't your highest, is the most important. Dr. Glasser taught that you realize all your other needs through your need for Connection; humans are hardwired for it. You need relationships in your life, and you need groups and places where you feel you belong. This is true for everyone, but there are some who need it more than others.

Do you like spending time with people? Are you someone who likes to help others? Are you a peacemaker, avoiding conflict whenever possible? Is giving and receiving love one of your favorite things to do? Are you in tune with others, being one of the first to notice when someone isn't quite right? Do you find you have deep, meaningful relationships? Are you someone that prioritizes people over most anything else? Then you might have a high need for Connection.

The need for Connection is about family, love, and friendship. It is about reaching out for those who build you up and validate you, while minimizing your connection with those who tear you down and discredit you. Connection is about affiliation, cooperation, sharing, and intimacy. Additionally, it's about feeling as though you truly belong.

When you feel unhappy, assess the level of Connection

157

you have in your life. Needing Connection will often result in feeling isolated, lonely, unwanted, or disconnected from the people important to you. How would you assess the level of Connection in your life right now? Do you have too little, too much, or just the right amount?

Even if you have a low need for Connection, it can become a priority when it isn't being met. If you find yourself alone a lot of the time unintentionally, don't feel you fit in anywhere, are being bullied, or just believe people don't like you for whatever reason, you will probably experience a push to meet your need for Connection. It's not that the need has grown stronger, you are just having a more difficult time meeting it.

As with the four previous needs, it's also possible to have more Connection than you actually need in your life, making it challenging to meet your other needs. If the people in your life all want your attention, you may feel overwhelmed. You might be exhausted from trying to fix everyone's problems and conflicts. You may miss your privacy if there are people constantly around you, craving some alone time to get your thoughts together. With too much Connection, you put others before yourself. Your need for Significance will be compromised when you prioritize people over what you want to accomplish. You may ignore what's necessary to protect yourself to satisfy someone else, such as having unprotected sex. You can compromise Joy to fulfill a Connection request, such as taking care of an elderly parent every moment of your spare time.

Whether you have too much or too little Connection, ask yourself these questions: Are your relationships with the important people in your life satisfactory? Is your life as conflict-free as possible? Are you setting reasonable boundaries with people? Do you get enough Freedom while also meeting your need for Connection? Are you trying to mold people into someone you want them to be? Are you holding grudges?

When you need more Connection in your life, you might consider spending time with your friends, calling a supportive family member, or spending time with children or pets. Alternatively, you might want to go where you are appreciated and feel like you belong—maybe the bowling league, your place of worship, the gym, or the local club—wherever people know and relate with you. You may also decide to work on that all-important relationship you have with the *most* important person in your life—YOU!

The Connection need shares a complex and often inverse relationship with the Freedom need. It's common that a high need for one results in a low need for the other, but this is not always the case. Having high needs for both means you will have to discover ways to be free either within your relationships or outside of them.

Other priorities may cause you to temporarily put Connection on the back burner: a project that must be done, errands you've been putting off, or an obligation you must fulfill. However, as with every need, once your levels of Connection reach an unhealthy level, you will feel driven to do something about it.

When you have responsible ways to connect, you will choose them; if none are available and the call for Connection is strong, you will grasp any means available to you. This can manifest as promiscuous sexual behavior, neediness with others, and manipulative behavior to get others to "like" you. These less responsible ways of meeting the Connection need damages the relationship you have with your Self.

On the surface, this need may seem dependent on other people. It is not! When you are missing love in your life, it is time to be more loving. Find others that would want your help and volunteer your services. Find people who are also looking for Connection and be their friend. Adopt a pet, though if you're seeking Connection, I recommend a dog. Dogs *always* want Connection, unlike other pets; it's incredibly heartbreaking, but they will even love an owner who mistreats them. If none of these options are currently available to you, you can always work to improve the connection you have with your Self.

You may try to compensate for your lack of Connection by filling up in other areas. Using Significance, Joy, Safety & Security, or Freedom to fill up your Connection need won't work.

When you need Connection, it is only through Connection that this need will be satisfied. For example, some people who look for Connection will use power, manipulation, and control to force what they want from a relationship. While it may meet the need for Significance, it will never improve their Connection.

When you have a healthy amount of Connection in your life, you will feel good about your relationships. You have discovered the right amount of time to spend with people, managed the conflicts in your life, and learned to appreciate what you have.

You may have some rules that prevent you from connecting with others. A client of mine felt her children and grandchildren should call her more often, and she made herself miserable wondering why they didn't phone more frequently. I asked if she had considered phoning them and she said, "Oh, I couldn't do that. They are so busy." She wanted to have relationships with her family but told herself she couldn't initiate that connection. She will remain lonely and disconnected until she gives herself permission to originate contact with her family or meets other people she can connect with. By doing neither up to this point, she set herself up for total frustration.

Perception can shape the Connection need. You tend to make up stories in your head about people and the relationships you have with them. Sometimes you might perceive you have a closer relationship than you do; other times, you may perceive someone doesn't like you when they actually do. When relationships end, you create a perception about the reason why and usually that perception doesn't serve you.

A good way to check your perceptions is to ask your Self, "Is the way I'm thinking about this connection helping me or preventing me from being the person I want to be?" If your perception is hurting you, then you have the power to change it! It's your story, so write one that supports you; free yourself from your harmful perceptions and nurture that important relationship with your Self.

In her book, *Love for No Reason*, Marci Shimoff writes about the comfort zone people construct around the concept of love and relationships. This is where they develop the level of satisfaction and love they believe they are entitled to in relationships. When you start to feel happier than you think you deserve, you will likely do something to sabotage that relationship. We will explore this idea of the comfort zone later in this chapter.

The areas I consider part of the Connection need are your relationship with your sexuality, the relationship you have with your expectations, and your relationship with the concept of love.

The relationship you have with your sexuality will help you be able to enjoy and participate in sexual activity either by yourself or with a partner. The relationship you have with your expectations determines how you allow other people to affect you. Finally, the relationship you have with the concept of love is critical to how you move through the world and connect with others. What are your beliefs about love—not just love with other people, but also with loving your Self?

In order to be a need-satisfying person in your own Quality World, being aware of where you stand with your Connection need is one more piece to the overall puzzle of loving yourself. Other people will come and go, but you will always remain. Become a person you love to hang out with, and you will never be lonely again. Let's look at how you can accomplish that.

RELATIONSHIP WITH YOUR SEXUALITY

"Don't knock masturbation. It's sex with someone I love." — Woody Allen

When you have a healthy, positive relationship with your Self, you know and love your Self sexually. Societal norms have made this quite difficult, as many of us were told at an early age sexuality is "dirty." Growing up, I remember mothers telling their sons they risked blindness by touching their penis; little girls are often told touching themselves is "dirty," "bad," or "unladylike." Some religions tell their followers that sex is sinful unless done within the institution of marriage. In addition, a person who is gay, lesbian or bisexual may be told that sexual activity between two persons of the same gender is wrong or sinful. Members of the LGBTQ community are often told their sexual orientation or identity is wrong, sinful, and in severe cases, an outright abomination. When it comes to sexuality, is it any wonder people grow up not knowing who they are, what they like, and what they don't?

For those who have been sexually assaulted, there is information in this chapter that may bring you back to that painful time. It's understandable if you want to skip this section, but if not, breathe your way through it—stop and return as often as it takes to process the information. Someone used you, hurt you, and devalued you—understand that you did nothing wrong. The shame is theirs, not yours. I hope you will continue reading so you can make peace with yourself. This section will help you begin to see your body and sexuality as the healthy and wonderful gift it is.

In my early counseling career, I spent a lot of time working with sexually abused children. I noticed three separate responses to this abuse. Some children became sexually active with multiple partners, learning to use sex to get what they want or confusing it with love. Some children became sex avoidant, using multiple layers of clothing or excess weight to disguise their sexuality, attempting to make themselves unattractive to sexual predators. The third group attempted to use denial, acting as if nothing had happened in hopes no one would ever find out or realize there was something "different" about them.

Most studies agree that one in three girls will be sexually abused prior to her eighteenth birthday. For boys, depending on the study, it is one in six or seven. If you are a survivor of sexual abuse, it may be more challenging for you to know yourself sexually; your perceptions about love and sex have been heavily influenced by those who abused your body and your vulnerability.

That does not mean you cannot heal. If you are still feeling the effects of past abuse, reach out to a recommended mental health professional who specializes in trauma care. If the first therapist you see is not helpful, keep trying until you find a person you're comfortable with and able to complete the necessary work with to begin healing.

Whether or not you have experienced sexual abuse, you have learned about your body in various ways—some of them healthy, some not. In an effort to create a healthy relationship with your Self and your sexuality, you will want to affirm your sexual/affectional orientation. There are many sexual/affectional orientations, including heterosexual, homosexual, bisexual, and asexual. Who you choose to be sexual with may not always match your sexual/affectional orientation. Your orientation encompasses who you love in all ways—not only physically and sexually, but also mentally, spiritually, emotionally, and psychologically. Your choice of a sexually intimate partner may differ from that at times during your life. The people you are attracted to and fall in love with are not believed to be something you choose. However, you can choose who you want to be sexual with. You need to give yourself permission to participate in sexual behavior with a receptive partner of your choosing.

Having a healthy relationship with your sexuality will provide clarity about the who, what, when, and where of sexual activity, as well as the level of your willingness to experiment and try new things: who you're attracted to, what you like and dislike, how often you want to be sexual, and where you're comfortable being sexual.

To determine whether your preferences and habits are of your own desires or instilled in you by others, ask yourself the questions from Chapter Two. Let's look at these answers from the perspective of one of my clients.

She believes, "Masturbation is wrong. It's dirty to touch yourself. Sex is a duty women perform for their husbands." Her answers follow:

1. Where did that come from? *My mother and probably her mother before that, on and on for generations.*
2. Did I trust and respect the person? *Yes*

3. Did I believe that person had my best interest at heart? *Yes*

4. Were they right? *No*

5. How do I know? *Masturbation isn't wrong. It is a way to pleasure myself and help me understand what I like.*

6. Where did my mother get her information? *Probably her mother.*

7. Is it a truth for her that isn't necessarily a truth for me? *I'm thinking this may not even be true for my mother. She has accepted it as truth from her mother.*

8. Is this information that serves me and makes me stronger or does it belittle me and make me weaker? *This information does not serve me or make me stronger. In fact, it causes me to dislike something that's supposed to be beautiful.*

9. What do I want to be true? *I want to be comfortable and confident in using self-pleasuring to achieve orgasm and to explore what I like and don't like during intimacy.*

10. What steps do I need to take to make it so? *I need to be loving with myself and fully present in the moment. I need to quiet the critical voice in my head by concentrating on the physical sensations and creating positive, loving statements instead. I need to be committed enough to work through the discomfort and continue to practice until I get more comfortable with it.*

After freeing yourself from the messages of others, however well intentioned, you will be free to explore your sexuality to determine what you like and what you don't. Self-pleasure is an important part of this process. If you still have the perspective that masturbation is not appropriate for you, then you might not want to experiment with yourself. If this is your decision, based on your values and beliefs, then you may prefer experimenting with a partner to determine your likes and dislikes.

If your values and beliefs support your willingness and desire to self-pleasure then, to echo the Woody Allen quote in the beginning of the chapter, think of this activity as having sex with someone you love. There are many options for masturbation and self-exploration that can be found in boutiques, adult stores, catalogues, home parties, and even on Amazon. Buying adult "toys" can be expensive, so if you have any friends you are comfortable speaking with first, get their opinion on which toy might be best to start with. Salespeople in adult stores can also be helpful in terms of choosing what might suit you best.

Why do you want to do this? There are many reasons, but the first one is to learn to love yourself through stimulation of your body. Secondly, an orgasm is an effective way to reduce stress and promote relaxation. Thirdly, for several women, self-pleasure is the only way they achieve orgasm.

In 2015, Cosmopolitan conducted a survey with 2,300 women ages eighteen to forty and learned that 39% of the women surveyed reach their orgasms by masturbating with their hand or a sex toy. Knowing the mechanics of your own body is good in and of itself, but it will also be helpful if you want to teach sexual partners how to pleasure you, increasing the likelihood that you will better enjoy intimate time with them.

When you decide to explore your body sexually, take your time. Make it an event, not something to hurry through. Treat yourself as well as you would your lover. Light the candles, put on some romantic music, plug in your diffuser, and make love to the one you love most—you!

Exploring your sexuality through self-pleasuring may be awkward at first, not unlike your first experience with a sexual partner. Be patient with yourself. Tune in to the sensations of your body rather than focusing on achieving orgasm. It's okay if the orgasm doesn't happen for you the first few times; don't become frustrated. Enjoy the positive feelings you did create and make another date with yourself to try again.

Your body was made to be explored and enjoyed. Your skin is the largest organ of your body and, while it has a protective purpose, it can be a great source of pleasure. There are many things you can do to explore your body by simply exposing your skin to different stimuli—cotton, silk, lotion, oil, and feathers, to name a few.

The clitoris contains at least eight thousand sensory nerve endings, while the penis has about four thousand. This is the highest concentration of nerves anywhere in the body, making these sex organs extremely sensitive—start with gentle pressure until you know what your body can handle.

Even though there are always things you can improve about your body, do not focus on that during intimate moments: be mindful, connect with your physical Self, and appreciate the body you have. Be romantic—imagine the things you would want a lover to say to you and then say them to your Self. Touch your body in the way you would like a sensitive, loving partner to touch you. Try different pressure and experiment with new things.

Your goal doesn't have to be orgasm, but simply to feel good. If orgasm is your goal, keep practicing as many times as it takes to reach climax. It may not happen the first time, the second, or third, but be patient, take your time, and always love yourself through it. Your goal is to get to know your body and what you like. Even if you never communicate what you learn to a sexual partner, you get to do this for your Self.

If you choose to do your sexual exploration with a partner, that works too! I recommend exploring your body alone, so you aren't thinking about whether what you're doing is satisfying to your partner. You are in total control of what is happening with yourself. When you opt to do the sexual exploration with a partner, you will want to:

1. Choose a partner interested in your exploration and satisfaction.
2. Develop clear and satisfying communication during intimacy that doesn't come across as impatient or critical.
3. Silence the voice inside your head that might be reminding you about the cellulite you have on

your thighs or that chocolate mousse you had for dessert by mindfully zeroing in on the physical sensations occurring in your body. Whenever your mind wanders, just as in meditation, gently bring it back to the current moment and the feelings you are experiencing.

4. Sex with a partner involves give and take, but when you are exploring your sexuality, it might be good to have an agreement with your partner about taking turns so one of you is being satisfied exclusively and then the other gets his or her turn. This way you can completely concentrate on your experience, rather than be concerned about simultaneously satisfying your partner.

5. Be willing to experiment; don't decide you don't like something without trying it first. It's a little like when your parents said you had to at least try your Brussell sprouts before deciding you didn't like them. Be open to trying new things with a generous spirit.

6. Respect your partner's likes and dislikes. When either of you has tried and doesn't like something, then respect that boundary and work on finding something else that will satisfy you both.

When you were a child, the connection you had with your body was how you learned to distinguish yourself from the rest of the world. You learned where you ended and everything else began by touching yourself, realizing touching other things felt different. Part of creating a healthy relationship with your sexuality is to:

- Examine the values and beliefs you have around your sexuality.
- Let go of the values and beliefs that no longer serve you.
- Develop new affirmations about your sexuality.
- Explore your body.
- Become clear about what you like and don't like.

- Communicate your preferences to anyone with whom you engage in intimate activity.

Having an aware, willing, and loving relationship with your sexuality will always serve you, whether you are single or in a relationship, and it will help you better connect with your partner when engaging in sexual activity. The mental constructions you've fabricated over the years about sexuality is where the challenge lies, and not in the actual mechanics of being sexual with yourself or with a partner. Check where your unloving thoughts, beliefs, and values around sexuality came from, and replace them with healthy thoughts, beliefs, and values through patient, loving exploration.

RELATIONSHIP WITH YOUR EXPECTATIONS

"No one has ever broken your heart. They broke your expectations. And by breaking your expectations they helped you get closer to your heart."
– Kyle Cease

Expectations are a complex thing. I have heard it said to hope for the best but plan for the worst; some would say if your expectations are too low, that is exactly what you'll get. Henry Ford said, "If you think you can do a thing or think you can't do a thing, you're right." The discriminating difference is whether you are having expectations of yourself or other people.

Since you control your actions and most of your thoughts, you are entitled to set whatever expectations you want for your Self. However, every time you set expectations for the other people in your life, you set yourself up for disappointment. Of course, sometimes people will meet and even exceed your expectations, but the possibility always exists that they won't. When they don't, you might be tempted to accuse them of breaking your heart when, in reality, *you* set yourself up for the disappointment.

The one thing you can expect from other people is that they'll do whatever best suits their needs at the time, and you shouldn't want them to do any differently. Your best bet is to ask people for what you want, but have several backup plans. At least one of these plans should depend solely on yourself, without depending on the responses or actions of others, or perhaps a professional whose livelihood depends on performing what you need.

When creating a healthier relationship with your Self, it's important to manage your expectations of others. To accomplish this, we'll tackle it piece by piece: setting boundaries, managing your emotions, practicing acceptance, extending forgiveness, and maintaining gratitude. Setting boundaries allows you to use the time you have for what's important to you, rather than what's important to others. Your emotions can sometimes take priority over logic, so learning to recognize and understand your emotions is important to this conversation. You may need to learn to accept people, including yourself, for who they are; forgive them and yourself for any perceived shortcomings or any wrongs that have been done. Finally, a huge task of one's relationship with Connection is to practice gratitude for the wonderful, the painful, the sticky, and the unfinished—all of it!

SETTING BOUNDARIES

"Guilt can prevent us from setting the boundaries that would be in our best interests, and in other people's best interests." – Melody Beattie

Setting boundaries with people, places, and things is the first step toward managing your expectations. Your life is in a state of constant flux, and maintaining balance is of paramount importance. Naturally, you won't be completely balanced all of the time, but being aware of your balance, or lack thereof, is the first step to creating boundaries.

Here are some questions to consider in this area: Am I in balance now? If I agree to this person, place, or thing will I be able to maintain or create better balance in my life? Will agreeing establish a challenge for me in getting what I want and need?

When you agree to do something you really don't want to

do, you are denying yourself what is most important to you. You might think you're doing a good thing by helping someone else meet their needs, but the reality is, you cannot meet someone else's needs for them. All you can do is provide opportunities another person can choose to meet their own needs—that is your part of the equation. It is always your responsibility to get your own needs met, not someone else's. Conversely, you cannot meet someone else's needs for them. This is why setting boundaries is so important; they are barriers put in place to keep you safe, protect your time and priorities, and maintain your healthy balance.

As a person with a very high need for Connection, setting boundaries is not something that comes easily to me. If someone calls me and wants help with a particular situation, I'm very likely to drop whatever I'm doing so I can be of service. This may sound selfless to an outside observer, but it actually serves my desire to help and make connections. Times when it wouldn't serve me is when I am asked to bake for a bake sale (I don't like doing that), donate to causes that aren't important to me, or accompany someone to a place I really don't want to go. Do you ever do that?

One day, I was planning to fly from Tucson to Pittsburgh with a three and a half hour layover in Chicago. I texted a good friend of mine to see if he wanted to meet me for dinner, and he replied he was unable to because he had some long overdue yard work to complete. At first I was stunned, thinking, *Well, I must not be very important to you. I would never prioritize yard work over time with you!* I then remembered times I have prioritized people over tasks to get done, which consequently left me scrambling and stressed, completing what needed to be done in a compressed timeframe. This was meant to be a cosmic lesson for me: my friend wasn't saying no to me, but yes to himself.

Whenever you're asked to do something, determine if it's something you really want to do, or something you're tempted to do just to avoid conflict or another's disappointment. Sacrificing what you really want to do for someone else's happiness has the potential to create serious imbalance for you. Perhaps using an excuse or lie to get out of going will pile on serious guilt for you, and while being honest may hurt the other person, remember it's their responsibility to meet their needs, not yours. It can be a hard decision to say no to someone you like and respect while saying yes to your Self, but who are you in relationship with for your entire life? Yes, you! That's the number one relationship you need to nourish, for the sake of your own mental and emotional health.

There are likely people in your life who are toxic for you; whenever you are with them, they are energy vampires, so it's critical to set strict boundaries with them. They can drain your energy, or worse—rob you of your positivity. An unknown individual wisely quipped, "Standing alone is better than standing with people who don't value you," and I would add, "or your time." So, what can you do? A Choice Theory colleague of mine, Ellen Gélinas, does a humor workshop, and in it she advises to boldly and honestly say, "I'm sorry, but that just won't fit in my schedule." Another answer could be, "I'm very sorry, but I just have too much on my plate right now to take on one more thing."

If you want to reduce time spent with toxic people, simply become too busy to see them. Be clear about how much time, if any, you are going to give this person. If it is a peripheral person in your life, you can probably cut them out completely. If it is someone closer, you may need to be very clear with yourself, *I'll give this person three hours a week of my time and that's all.* If you choose the latter, consider what need you meet when you agree to spend that time.

We never actually do anything we don't *want* to do. When you choose to give even a second of the 31,536,000 seconds you have each year to a toxic person, how does that actually benefit you? Why do you choose it? Why do you *want* to? Does it meet your need for Connection? Safety & Security? Significance? I doubt it meets your needs for Freedom or Joy, but consider those as well. When you are clear about what you gain from giving time to toxic people, then determine if doing

171

so helps you improve the relationship you have with the most important person in your life—YOU!

Once you have that answer, see if you can figure out a way to have both—a positive relationship with your Self and the benefit you receive from donating your time to toxic people. If there is, create it. If not, evaluate which is more important—the benefit, or the relationship you have with your Self. Since you are reading this book, I already know you are at least considering *Choosing Me Now*, so make a plan that reduces time with toxic people and replaces what you lose by doing so.

EMOTIONS, ACCEPTANCE, FORGIVENESS & GRATITUDE

"Relinquishing the delusional hope that we can or must be flawless – allows us to seek happiness in the only place it can be found: our real, messy, imperfect experience." – Martha Beck

Universal balance is the only perfection that exists, yet somehow, either from external factors or your own expectations, you got the message you are supposed to be perfect. Whenever something happens that upsets the balance of our world, the Universe goes into overdrive to restore it.

As part of the Universe, you have an inherent, internal drive to maintain your personal balance. It's not just mentally, but physically as well: white blood cells rush to infection sites to restore balance, your body craves certain foods when you have a vitamin deficiency, and your mind demands sleep when you have been too busy or restless.

When you are out-of-balance, the Universe has to work harder to maintain overall universal balance. Where there is tragedy, there is triumph. Where there is hate, there is love. When there is destruction, there is creation. When humans destroy the environment, the Universe responds with ways to right the wrong; if the destruction is so vast, extinction may be necessary to restore the balance.

Indeed, universal balance is the only perfection that exists in the world. You can choose to contribute to or take away from the balance; you can have a positive universal affect, or you can cause other measures to take place to restore the balance you've disrupted. You can allow your emotions to control your behavior, or you can use your emotions as a tool to recognize your own imbalance and how you can restore it. You can learn to accept, forgive, and appreciate, or you can hold grudges that nurture hatred in your heart. Let's look at how to let go of the things in your life that destroy balance and implement those that will contribute to it instead.

EMOTIONS

Mike Dooley, owner of Thoughts Become Things (*www. tut.com*), writes, "Choose feelings over logic, adventure over perfection, here over there, now over then, and always love, love, love." This sums up the essence of letting go of what doesn't work to make room for what does.

Your feelings provide information about whether you're getting what you want, but you can override those feelings by misusing logic, convincing yourself to accept anything. Choosing here over there is about appreciating where you are at any given point in time; now over then is to embrace the present moment, while allowing our memories a place in your heart; and putting love into the world is so much better than its alternative—you become part of the solution instead of the problem.

Knowing and understanding Choice Theory psychology does not mean you will never again experience anger, frustration, disappointment, sadness, jealousy, or any other painful emotion. I'm clearly not recommending that you feel the "dreaded emotion" and then frantically work to stop feeling it—that would be suppressing your emotions, and I don't support that as a standard or healthy practice. Stuffing emotions down inside and repressing them leads to suffering of mass proportions.

Emotions are energy. *All About Science* (*https://goo.gl/fNQNwr*) writes on its website:

> In its simplest form, the First Law of Thermodynamics states that neither matter nor

energy can be created or destroyed. The amount of energy in the universe is constant—energy can be changed, moved, controlled, stored, or dissipated. However, this energy cannot be created from nothing or reduced to nothing. Every natural process transforms energy and moves energy, but cannot create or eliminate it.

Energy that enters a system must either be stored there or leave. When experiencing the energy of an emotion you do not want, it will either be stored in your body somewhere or leave your system. You can't force it out by denying, repressing, or ruminating over it. You can help it leave by talking about it, writing about it, exercising it out, or changing your actions and thoughts to create a different energy.

When the world doesn't match up to what you want or expect, you will have a visceral response. You want it to change into the way you want it to be. This is the human condition. You can mitigate this sometimes by working on the things you want and the expectations you have for situations and other people. Expecting things from other people often leads to disappointment. Other people are trying to live up to their own expectations—it's exhausting having to live up to the expectations you have for them as well.

These are some examples of broken expectations I have heard in my sessions:

1. I wanted an engagement ring; I got a Pandora bracelet.
2. I wanted my son to make honor society; he came home with three Cs on his report card.
3. I wanted to go out to eat and all my husband could say was, "What's for dinner?"
4. At the end of the day when we went to bed, I wanted to make love to my wife but she told me she was too tired.

When expectations are broken and desires frustrated, you are going to experience a painful emotion. That signal is something you want to register; you want to experience it, while simultaneously asking your Self, "What's happening right now in this moment?"

Being upset with your boyfriend for not being where you are about marriage isn't realistic. Being angry with your child for not matching your academic expectations isn't healthy. Being angry your husband didn't read your mind and offer to take you to dinner isn't productive. Feeling frustrated your wife isn't interested in sex doesn't help. However, you still experience those emotions, so what do you do with them?

The first step is to objectively study them—ask your Self, "*What am I feeling and why?*" You are feeling upset, angry, disappointed, or frustrated because you are not getting what you want. This emotion is signaling that something isn't the way you want it to be, and concurrently, it is an indicator that you are using this emotion to get what you want.

When I asked my son to clean up his room and he responded with, "I'll do it after I finish this game." *Fine,* and then when one game leads to another, and then another, and I ask again. He says, "I'll do it right after this TV show is over." *OK, fine,* but then he still doesn't, and as the day goes on, I feel my frustration building because I wanted it done the first time I asked. As the dinner hour approaches, at my wits end, I scream at my son, "Will you just clean up your room already?" As an untrained observer, you might say my son "made" me angry, but people who practice Choice Theory psychology know I am using my anger as my best attempt to get my son to do what I want. That may sound like semantics, but it is important to reiterate as we move forward to what I call transmuting your painful emotions.

When you realize your emotions are both a sign you're not getting what you want and the way you think you can get what you want, you are ready to process them. First comes the signal, and you notice, *Oh isn't that interesting, I'm feeling frustrated, annoyed, agitated because what I want most right now isn't happening.* Use mindful focus to zero in on that energy in your body. What does it feel like? Where is it located? Breathe through it. Be the Watcher by noticing, *This is interesting. I wonder what I am creating this emotion for?*

It's not always easy to pinpoint the goal of an emotion because it requires a huge shift from the faulty belief that emotions just happen. They don't just happen—you create them to help you get what you want. Going back to those earlier scenarios, the woman who created disappointment with her Pandora bracelet was attempting to let her boyfriend know she was expecting something else without coming right out and saying so. The parent upset with his son's grades created anger to let his son know he better prioritize his grades next time. The woman disappointed her husband didn't read her mind and take her to dinner was trying to let him know how much she needs his understanding and appreciation. The man who was frustrated with his wife for not fulfilling his sexual desires was sending a message to her that he wants her to respond to his sexual advances.

When you are working on letting go of what doesn't work, you need to tune into the subconscious emotional blackmail you may engage in with those close to you. Strong emotions are not something you can easily hide from others. Emotions have energy, and that energy can be felt, read, and misinterpreted by those around you.

When you support the people in your life making their own decisions based on what meets their needs, you will talk to your Self whenever you are experiencing strong emotions to the contrary. Try to identify the goal you want to accomplish by using those emotions. Once you recognize it, you can remind yourself that other people have the right to make the decisions that are best for them. You might be able to provide them with information that will encourage them to choose the options you prefer, but you don't have the right to control or coerce anyone into doing things your way.

When you are clear about that, then look inside your Self to determine how best to proceed. There are three options that still may get you what you want. If none of those are successful, there's a consolation option, transmuting the emotion you don't want to be experiencing, that will at least help you feel better and an independent option that will never fail you.

If asking for what you want doesn't work, then you can look at any of these three options on their own or in combination with each other. One, you can decide to change what you want. Using the examples from earlier, you can decide you aren't ready to get married anyway, are focused more on your son's overall wellbeing than just his grades, want to eat at home to prepare a new recipe, and want to stay up late to watch the game tonight anyway.

Two, you can change your behavior or approach to getting what you want. When you realize disappointment isn't getting you the ring you want, you can ask your boyfriend his thoughts on taking your relationship to a deeper level. With your son, you could start talking to him about his goals and aspirations instead of micromanaging his grades, allowing him to draw his own conclusions about what grades he will need. With your husband, you may provide him with a list of options for eating out. With your wife, you could use romance to help her become more sexually receptive.

Three, you can change your story or your perception. In each example, you have written a story in your head. You told yourself your boyfriend doesn't want to get married, or worse, doesn't really love you, and that's why you didn't get the ring. You told yourself your son is never going to be a success if he can't control himself and do better with his grades. You told yourself your husband doesn't appreciate how hard you work every day. You told yourself your wife doesn't find you attractive anymore, doesn't love you, or must be getting sex from someone else! All of these are stories you have fabricated, and you have no idea if there is any truth to any of them.

As suggested in Chapter Two, it's time to write a new story. Tell yourself your boyfriend is taking the time he needs so that, when he's ready to make the commitment, the circumstances will be right. Tell yourself your son is capable of getting the grades he needs once he recognizes their importance, or that he knows how to get the help he needs to improve his grades.

Remind yourself that you never told your husband you wanted to eat out, and had he known, he would have gladly taken you to a restaurant. Remember all the work your wife does and that she has every reason to be tired and not in the mood.

The consolation option determines what need or needs would best be met if the other person did what you wanted. Once you have that answer, find other ways to meet that need.

Getting an engagemnt ring could meet many of your needs. You may want to feel more secure in the relationship, more connected to your boyfriend, or more significant to him. If your son earned higher grades, you might feel safer and more secure about his future, more significant because your child is doing well, or more connected because you would feel closer to him; it's possible you meet your needs for Freedom and Joy to do some things you want to do instead of spending your time and energy "helping" him get better grades. Going out to eat with your husband could help you feel connected, significant, and important in the relationship; you will be free from having to cook and get to enjoy a night out. Having sex with your wife could meet your need for Connection because you want to feel close to her, Significance because you want to be important to her, Joy for obvious reasons, and it might even help you feel more Secure in your relationship.

After determining which need or combination of needs you're trying to satisfy, develop a behavior that will meet those needs in a different way. Sometimes you have a strong Quality World picture that involves another person helping you meet your need. When that person doesn't want to match your Quality World picture, then you might fabricate a story that excuses you from meeting the need in another way. It's not true! Of course, you can meet that need—just probably not in the way you are imagining and not with the person you wanted.

Having the flexibility to adjust your Quality World to optimize success is one sign of a healthy relationship with your Self. Being inflexible with unwilling people will likely lead to disappointment for you or misery for the other person as you try to coerce him or her into doing what you want. The Rolling

Stones really said it best, "You can't always get what you want, but if you try sometimes, you just might find, you get what you need."

I'm not suggesting that you hurt your current relationships, but that you find another way to meet the need that feels most depleted. If you need more Connection, spend time with friends, pet the dog, or go visit a family member. If you need more Safety & Security, prepare for the worst case scenario, get an alarm system, or talk with someone you trust about your fears. If you want more Significance, complete a project or goal, spend time doing something you have total control over, or go somewhere you feel listened to and respected. If you need more Freedom in your life, go for a drive, do something outside your comfort zone, or do something by yourself you've always wanted to do. If you need more Joy, play in some way, relax, or learn something new.

The never fail, independent option to get more of what you need is to look inside your Self. The previous ideas work well when you have other options available to you, but what if you don't? Then you can find what you need inside your Self. Need more Safety & Security? Remember you are safe. Need more Significance? Remember you are important. Need more Freedom? Remember you are free in every important way. Need more Joy? Remember you are Joy—playful, relaxed and open to learning. Need more Connection? Remember you are connected and you are love. It's all inside you—you are complete; nothing is missing.

ACCEPTANCE

So much of our unhappiness comes from fighting reality. We want to change people and situations from what they actually are. One of my many mentors, Wayne Dyer, said, "Peace is the result of retraining your mind to process life as it is, rather than as you think it should be." If you could live in your Quality World, life would be great, but you don't get to live there. You need to deal with reality as it exists, despite whether or not it exists as you prefer.

179

When I think of acceptance, the Serenity Prayer comes to mind. It is actually repeated at the close of many twelve-step meetings, but Choice Theory people sometimes adjust the prayer just a bit to be more in line with what we teach. It goes like this:

God, grant me the serenity to accept the people I cannot change,
Courage to change the one I can,
And the wisdom to know that person is me.

Imagine the peace that would be yours if you actually lived your life in accordance with that principle. It's much easier to say than to do, but certainly is a goal to aspire to as you work on letting go of what doesn't work to make room for what does. Fighting reality won't work. What does work is adjusting your Self to accommodate the reality of your life.

Accept that what is happening is actually happening; it is your reality. There is no point in fighting it because it already exists. Go with it. You might be able to change the next moment, but the one you already find yourself in is what it is. Accepting, rather than fighting it, is the second step toward peace.

The next step is to objectively look at what you want. Be honest with yourself in this exploration. *What do I want and why is that important to me? What will it change?*

During this investigation, you may realize that what you want really isn't important. Through working with couples, I have discovered two specific and insignificant habits that are often the cause of animosity in the relationship. Often wives are upset with their husbands for leaving their dirty clothes on the floor in front of the hamper. Husbands often complain about being met with a nearly empty fuel tank whenever getting in their wife's car. In the grand scheme of things, are these problems important? Not really.

You may think you want something for someone else so much because it will make his or her life easier. Consider how valid your reasons are for wanting what you want, and you may recognize that the person you want this for couldn't care less. This can help dissipate the anger, frustration, resentment, and disappointment.

If in the exploration of what you want you realize, *I DO really want this and there is nothing wrong with my wanting it. My reasons are valid and I plan to continue to strive toward what is important to me.* With this important realization, you recognize that you have the right to want whatever you want. You do not have to restrict your Self. *I have the right to want this!* Yes, you do!

You also have the right to adjust or change what you want for the greater good. For example, if you want something from someone else that he or she is unwilling to give, you definitely have the right to still want it. With the right information, reward, or punishment, you may be able to force it from them, but at what cost? Will it be worth it? Getting what you want in this way may sometimes cost you your relationship with that person, or worse, the relationship you have with your Self. Perhaps the greater good would be best served by changing what *you* want to preserve your relationship with others and your Self.

If you continue to want what you want, check in again to identify the feelings associated with that. If you are holding onto the pain, anger, frustration, or resentment, it has moved beyond being a mere signal of not getting what you want to something you are using as your best attempt to get what you want.

You are no longer experiencing frustration as a signal, but you are actually creating and maintaining it as your best attempt toward getting what you want. If you are sad enough, your partner might feel guilty and give you what you want. Creating anger may intimidate the other person into giving you what you want. Maintaining frustration may motivate you into working harder to get what you want. Ask your Self, "What am I trying to get with this emotion? How is it serving me? What possible benefit do I obtain from it?"

Once you recognize this emotion is a choice, an attempt to get what you want, then you can choose differently if you want to. To want to make a different choice, you must identify a better way. If something is working for you, no matter how marginally, it is difficult to choose something else without a sense that it will work even better. Critically analyze whether using this emotion to get what you want is the way you *really* want to do it. Often when you use your emotions, you aren't consciously aware you are doing so. Making it conscious helps you decide if you want to continue on that path or try something else.

Breaking my ankles in that hot air balloon accident is one of the best examples I have of this. When we landed on the ground and I realized I had broken my ankles, I had a signal of frustration. *This isn't what I want. I want to be able to leave Arizona and go home today.* Almost simultaneously, I had the thought, *Well, Kim, now you get the opportunity to practice what you preach.* Once I had that thought, the disappointment went away. I was able to focus on practicing Choice Theory in that situation. Was I suppressing my anger and disappointment? Not at all; those emotions were replaced with productive thoughts and emotions that supported my new goal.

Understanding your emotions and how they work is a process. Your feelings are always telling you something about what you want and how successful you are in getting it, but sometimes it can be difficult to figure out exactly what your feelings are saying to you.

Clearly, you have a right to feel anything you want to feel for as long as you want to feel it. I have a friend whose brother committed suicide two years ago. She knows Choice Theory but actively grieves for him every day. I attempted to help her move past the pain but she wants to still feel it; the pain seems to keep her brother alive in her heart and demonstrates how much she loved him. If she "moves on" too quickly, what might that say about her love? The pain isn't holding her back, rather it is how she chooses to get through the grief. She has the right to stay there as long as she wants.

However, if you are experiencing an emotion you'd like to let go of, this process might work for you:

1. Recognize and fully experience the emotional signal that you aren't getting what you want.
2. Accept the reality of the situation—what you want most right now isn't happening.
3. Define exactly what it is you want that you aren't

getting.

4. Ask your Self, "What does this actually mean to me? Is it really that important?"

5. Determine how you are using this emotion to try to get what you want.

6. Decide if that's the best way or if you want to try something different.

FORGIVENESS

Forgiveness can come from an apology, from a distance, and from within. When someone hurts you in some way, you perceive there has been an injury to you and the perpetrator needs to make amends somehow.

When the person issues a heartfelt apology, it's relatively easy to forgive. The bigger question is, can you forgive without an apology? What if the person isn't even aware of what they did? What if the person believes he has done nothing wrong? How do you forgive him? When you are harboring resentment against yourself or someone else, it's helpful to remember this bit of wisdom from Don Miguel Ruiz: "The good news is that nothing you [or anyone] have done is unforgivable. Such an act does not exist."

When you find holding onto the offense hurts you more than the other person, rise above the situation and let it go— forgive and move on. In this case, forgiving doesn't necessarily mean you repair the relationship, although you can. More often what happens is you will forgive from a distance. You recognize the other person was doing the best they knew to do under the circumstances and you forgive. You may still choose to no longer associate with that person, as you trust them to be the person they've already shown you they are, until they show you something different.

The most important way to forgive is in forgiving yourself for any grievances you believe you may have committed. It's easy to look back in hindsight and imagine a million ways to handle something differently but, as Choice Theory teaches, you did the best you knew at that point in time. Know that, forgive yourself, and do better next time.

Beating yourself up is not helping you. You may believe it helps prevent a recurrence, but think about it… if you don't want a friend to repeat a mistake, do you think constantly reminding her is the best way to proceed? No, a person needs acceptance, support, and encouragement, and so do you! Treat yourself as well as you would your best friend, because after all, you really are your own best friend.

Let go of regrets, recognize the lessons you've learned, and utilize the new information to do better in the future.

GRATITUDE

When I wrote my book, *Leveraging Diversity at Work*, I developed a Diversity Staircase that translated to the Relationshipping Staircase in *Secrets of Happy Couples*.

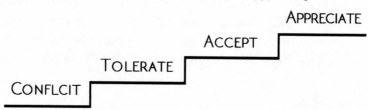

On the topic of gratitude, this stairway can be applied to your relationship with your Self. If something happened that you believe has negatively impacted you, or if you've done something you think is unforgivable, you are in conflict. Since being in conflict is benefiting you in some way, the first step to resolving it is deciding you want to, and then you can advance from conflict to tolerate what happened. Toleration isn't the end result you want to achieve. If someone told you they would "tolerate" you, it doesn't feel very good, but it is better than conflict. To tolerate is to not like what's happening but you're willing to stop fighting it. You're still unhappy, but you're putting up with it.

Beyond toleration is acceptance; you come to understand you have no right to change another person. When creating a healthy relationship with your Self, you accept the parts of yourself you may not like. Acceptance means letting go of the need to change things you've done but wished you hadn't. The painful emotions around the experience fall away, and you are at peace, understanding the past cannot be changed. Acceptance snuffs out the negativity; it feels so good that many people are happy to stay right there.

If you are willing, this one last step will take you to an even better place: appreciation. This requires finding the gift, lesson, or opportunity (GLO) in what began as conflict. Once you discover the positive balance of the negative event, you will find gratitude for having gone through what you originally felt conflicted over. This powerful exercise can change your life.

Elizabeth Lesser, the co-founder and senior advisor of Omega Institute wrote, "The changes I feared would ruin me have always become doorways, and on the other side I have found a more courageous and graceful Self." And Mike Dooley says, "There will always be people in your life who hold you back, who cost you too much, and who fail to see all you've done for them. But, of course, they're just there to teach you that you do have time, that you'll always be rich, and that your own high standards are all that matter."

The Universal Law of Attraction says you attract what you think about. When you are grateful for what you have, more positive things enter your life. I know someone who believes that no good deed goes unpunished and lives his life accordingly. Another person I know always claims she has the worst luck and nothing good happens to her. You know what? They are both right! The Universe delivers exactly what you expect. Other people can have similar "bad luck," persevere, and find the lesson in the situation, resulting in their happiness and contentment. From the outside looking in, they seem to lead charmed lives, but they are simply creating their reality just like those who expect negative outcomes do.

Gratitude also requires being thankful for what you have. Sheryl Crow sings, "It's not about having what you want; it's about wanting what you've got!" There is nothing wrong with wanting better for yourself as long as you remain grateful along the way.

Gratitude is the universal inoculation against anger, depression, jealousy, discontent, and boredom—really, any undesirable emotion you don't want to experience. Holding gratitude in your heart and mind pushes the negative out. You cannot be grateful and depressed at the same time. You can't feel gratitude and jealousy simultaneously. It's impossible to be grateful and angry or bored at the same time.

Giving yourself a daily dose of gratitude will improve your mental and emotional wellbeing; it's how I start my day. When I first wake up, I reflect on the things I get to do that day. I'll post that on Facebook, ending with the question, "What's great about your day?" It's my reminder to focus on what's special about my day and an invitation for my friends to do the same. When things may not be going the way I want, there is always something to be grateful for, even if it's just that I am breathing in and I am breathing out. I keep a Gratitude Journal, and at the end of the day, I record the the things that happened I'm grateful for. It is a planned practice of gratitude. Throughout my day, I try to notice those moments of gratitude, focus in on them and consciously soak it in. What is your gratitude practice each day?

RELATIONSHIP WITH THE CONCEPT OF LOVE

"Enjoy the love of others, but revel in the love of yourself. Don't wait for others to save you." – Aisha Tyler

What is your Connection with your past relationships? Do you have clean beginnings and endings? Do you stay in contact? Do you harbor animosity toward past loves and friendships? Your relationship with love may be healthy, dysfunction, or anywhere in between.

Based on what you've learned throughout your life, you write specific scripts on the many aspects of love: loyalty, commitment, friendship, parenting, and so on. You may not fully realize that these are unique to you, and others may not follow your script. What do you do when you become involved with someone with a different script? What does your script say about that?

What do you tell your Self about your Comfort Zone? Does fear of the unknown keep you there? Are you afraid to explore in a place that may be uncomfortable for you? Or do you fully embrace the unknown, striding straight ahead without considering the consequences? Is your Comfort Zone growing or shrinking? How do you feel about that? Who and what are responsible for these boundaries?

HEALTHY CONNECTIONS WITH YOUR PAST RELATIONSHIPS

"There are no wrong turns, only unexpected paths."– Mark Nepo

Do you have healthy connections with past relationships? Do you have difficulty letting go of relationships that are no longer working for you? Do you become impatient with people and walk away prematurely? All of us have prior relationships we may be holding onto in an unhealthy way. Feeling overly negative or overly positive toward someone from your past is typically a sign of an unhealthy connection.

When relationships end, they end for a reason. Sometimes that reason isn't of your choosing, and sometimes it is. How you manage your relationships with others is a reflection of how much you love and respect your Self. Nothing will deplete your self-esteem more than trying to hold on to someone who doesn't want you anymore. Yes, it's painful, and you may even feel so badly you want to die. However, if you want a healthier relationship with your Self, when relationships end, it's best to let them go gracefully.

Having either hatred or longing for someone from your past is a recipe for unhappiness. It's difficult to love yourself when you hold onto relationships that no longer serve you.

You can neutralize strong negative feelings with gratitude. Remember the positive parts of the relationship, and let them know they can spend time with whomever they want, even if it isn't you. Calling someone "my" boyfriend or "my" girlfriend implies possession. When we truly believe someone "belongs" to us, we are naturally upset if they choose to leave.

Know that whatever you did or didn't do in that relationship was a choice you made because it worked for you at the time. If you believed that your actions somehow obligated that person to you, you are mistaken. Even if there was explicit or implied agreement of obligation, people change their minds. Is it right? Is it fair? Either way, the important thing is that it *is*. Arguing with reality will only cause you unnecessary pain. Extend understanding, compassion, and forgiveness toward your ex. Continue healing and moving forward with someone new or on your own.

If you hold strong positive feelings for an ex and want them back in your life, decide if you want to express those feelings. If you're denied after asking once or twice, accept the reality of your life and move on. In this situation, I recommend a quotation by Dr. Seuss, "Don't cry because it's over; smile because it happened." For you to truly love yourself, you must stop longing for someone who no longer wants you.

When you love your Self, you won't want to keep putting yourself in situations where you feel rejected. You will surround your Self with people who encourage, support, and love you. If you believe this person only needs time before he or she returns to their senses and comes back to you, then give them the time and space they need to figure it out. In the meantime, live your life to its fullest.

After neutralizing your feelings about past relationships, you may choose to redefine that relationship. If you are both in agreement, a meaningful friendship may develop. You can also decide that, for your sanity, you need to no longer spend time with that person. Of course, you may define a relationship somewhere between those extremes. When you are no longer being held hostage by these feelings, you will move forward in a healthy way.

I consider myself a people collector. I maintain close friendships with most of the people I have had intimate relationships with. What helped me get to that place was remembering all the positivity from that relationship—lessons learned, fun times we had, positive emotions experienced, and gifts exchanged. I was able to put those relationships in their proper historical place while creating newfound friendships with my exes. However, there were two people from my past that, after neutralizing my feelings, I've decided to no longer associate with. They both took more than they gave in our relationships, and I had to care more about myself than I did them. When people from your past use, hurt, or abuse you, love your Self enough to close the door on that relationship and walk away.

Your Beliefs about Love

"I am love and as long as I seek it from you, I can't know that." – Byron Katie

Do you think you need to have a loving start in life to have the love you deserve? Do you believe you are somehow defective and don't deserve to be loved? Do you think you are half a person searching for your other half? Do you believe you need to give up what *you* want to make someone else happy? Do you prioritize those you love over everything else? Do you fear what will happen to you if someone stops loving you?

Your relationship with love has nothing to do with how many people you have in your life, the health of your relationship with a significant other, or the number of friends who adore you. These are byproducts of the relationship you have with love; love is about what you carry inside and project out to others.

The first step is knowing that you are not only worthy of love, you *are* love. Love is not something you have to go out and get or receive. Love always was and always will be inside you, no matter the circumstances of your birth, the relationship between your parents, or the details of your childhood.

Your parents may not have remembered that they too are love, and perhaps they were incapable of loving you the way you deserved. You can hold onto that injustice, or you can prevail in spite of it, understanding your parents did their best with the information available to them. It all depends on what you want and what you believe about love.

If you were shortchanged in the parenting department, search for other ways to fulfill the aspects of parenting you believe you missed out on. There are many surrogates, mentors, teachers, and coaches who are willing and able to re-parent you if you think that will be helpful, no matter your age.

In *Choosing Me Now*, you will need to remember you are love. Love is not something another person pours into you; you are not an empty vessel waiting for someone to fill you up— you are already full. You simply have to tune in, know you are worthy, and accept your birthright. You are love.

After accepting this truth, you become capable of oozing love out of every pore. You will know you are connected to everyone, realizing an unkindness toward anyone is an unkindness toward everyone. You will choose to be loving with everyone you know, and when you find that difficult, you might choose to distance your Self from that person, search diligently for something to like about him or her, or simply be kind anyway because that is who you want to be.

Not having a positive connection with love necessitates that you judge whether or not someone is worthy of your love or you are worthy of theirs. You withhold love in an attempt to get what you want, or you base your worth on whether others love you. These are all lies. True love is not conditional. Love begins in Spirit; love your Self, and love your Self deeply. From that foundation grows an appreciation and love for others, enabling you to tune into the connection between us all.

You came into this world as an innocent baby conceived in the love of the Universe; love your Self with that potential in mind. The experiences that made it either easy or difficult for you to believe you are love are behind you now.

Let go of those experiences, and adjust your thoughts on love. Love your Self the way you deserve to be loved, and give your Self the love you think you lacked. If others can't see the love you have inside of you, it's because they haven't yet found the love inside themselves. It is their deficit, not yours. However, when you are loving with people, they are often loving in return. This is a result of your living in love. It is not the *reason*. If you are loving toward people just to get love in return, your motive is impure and your love is conditional.

Living in love creates an abundance. You know you are already perfect; no one can steal your perfection. Even if you've done things you regret, you have learned from those things and know how to not repeat them. You realize you are a fully complete person; you do not have to give up your Self in order to be in a relationship, nor do you need another person to complete you.

When you are living in love, you may choose to share your life with another person, not because you need to but because you *want* to. You support and encourage your partner to do what he or she wants to do, as you also do for your Self. You do not have to give up what you want to ensure someone else's happiness. When you do something you know the other person will appreciate, you are giving from your heart while expecting nothing in return.

Never love someone more than you love yourself, because when you do, you allow things that don't work for you to operate against you. This is especially true when your non-negotiables are violated. Love your Self enough to walk away from toxic people. When you live in love, you will never fear the end of a relationship because you know all things have beginnings and endings. You are enough. You can sustain your Self and continue to love. It is who you are.

When you are loving for love's sake, you love unconditionally. This is a phrase that's constantly thrown around, but it truly means that you love without expecting one thing in return. It's a concept many of us strive for—unfortunately, most of us look to receive it rather than give it.

You do not simply love those that love you back or those you deem worthy. You love everyone because the alternative is unthinkable. You may love some from a distance, but you love nonetheless. You love because you *are* love. To do anything less defies Spirit and diminishes who you are and what you are here to do.

EXPANDING YOUR COMFORT ZONE

"Life begins at the end of your comfort zone." – Neale Donald Walsch

What is a comfort zone? How do you know if you're in it? How do you step out of it? How do you stay out of it? How do you become comfortable in your own skin?

The type of comfort zone you experience is correlated with your basic needs. If you have a high need for Safety & Security, then your comfort zone is constructed around safety issues. You'll know you've left it when you begin to feel nervous, anxious, or fearful.

If you have a high need for Significance, then your comfort zone is defined by power, importance, and respect. You know you have left your zone when you are experiencing disrespect, a lack of importance, and no power.

If you have a high need for Freedom, then your comfort zone is broad and the boundaries flexible. You know you have left your zone if you are feeling fenced in or trapped, with your back against a wall.

If you have a high need for Joy, then your comfort zone is comprised of play, relaxation, and/or learning. You will know you are out of your zone if you are experiencing boredom, exhaustion, or too much intense seriousness.

If you have a high need for Connection, then your comfort zone is comprised of relationships and connections. You will know you have left your zone when you are lonely and isolated, feeling adrift.

While all of this is true, it's not so simple. You are not one-dimensional, powered by one need alone. Sometimes your needs are in conflict with one other. Maybe you want more Connection at home while seeking more Significance at work. You might be willing to put your Safety & Security at risk to gain more Freedom in your life. Maybe you prioritize Safety & Security so much that your need for Connection suffers. There are all kinds of conflicts you deal with and manage every day.

There are basically two types of comfort zones. There are the comfort zones of your own choosing, based on knowledge, experience, and developmental stage. Then there are comfort zones that are created by the opinions of others; you may have blindly accepted boundaries or created them yourself out of fear, neither of which provide any sense of comfort. In the former, you experience no regret, no fear of missing out, nor longing for something more. In the latter, there will be a sense of frustration—whether obvious or barely perceptible, there's frustration nonetheless. You will desire more beyond the experience of safety and comfort you have constructed.

I had a male client who told his two daughters that they couldn't date until they turned thirty because men, excluding himself of course, are evil. I thought he was joking before realizing these were serious instructions given to his daughters. It is unsurprising that, at seventeen, the oldest had never been in a relationship, never been kissed, and had no desire to spend time with boys. These may be results of the "comfort" zone created by her father's warnings. She will stay safe there, but she won't fully live. It's very possible growing up this way may affect her relationships when she does turn thirty.

You may be living in your own fear-induced relationship "comfort" zone. You may be letting the excruciatingly painful end of a past relationship keep you from venturing into the dating arena. You spend your time alone or with friends, safe in your "comfort" zone. "*Nothing ventured, nothing gained*," became wisdom for a reason. Letting fear keep you in a "comfort" zone is not really living.

Compare and contrast that with being married, divorced, and creating a second marriage with the person of your dreams. You love one another deeply, can finish each other's sentences, and know each other's thoughts. You have never been more comfortable with another human being, and it feels like you've met your soul mate. This is a true comfort zone. It is based on experience, previous risk, and current happiness. I remember when my son wanted to settle in the place he grew up. I was fine with that decision, but I wanted him to live other places before staying in his hometown forever. I wanted his comfort zone to be a calculated construction rather than the simple default option—a comfort zone based on information instead of ignorance. For the rest of this section, we will discuss the "comfort zones" created by others, and those created from your own fear or ignorance.

Your comfort zone is actually bound by the beliefs, opinions, and rules you have made for yourself that help you feel safe and comfortable. While inside, it acts as a protective bubble, making certain you don't stretch too much, get out of line, or seek more than you believe you deserve. Being safe feels good; it feels like enough… only, it isn't.

Living in your comfort zone isn't really living at all; every day, you place a bet on a sure thing. There is no excitement in that—no risk, no learning, no freedom, no importance, no love. To truly live, you must step outside of this bubble. Staying inside may keep you safe, but at what cost? If you never risk anything, you never gain anything. Life becomes boring and meaningless. Outside, on the other hand, lies excitement. Making mistakes and failing teaches you something new. Outside, you can make an impact, a difference, a start to your legacy—but first, you must venture out. While trying to stay safe, you imprison yourself; step outside your comfort zone and experience what it is to be free from your fear. You're free to do whatever you want, only if you leave the safety of your bubble.

And it's outside that comfort zone where you will find *real* love. Maybe you're currently in a relationship that's within your comfort zone and feels safe to you. You know you won't get hurt, so you've settled for average or mediocre. Outside the comfort zone may lie your true love. You might even find it with your current partner, but you have to leave "safe" to find out.

Voices in your head will guide your steps; some will try to limit you and keep you safe, and others will encourage you to step out, try new things, and experience life in all its excitement. Listen to the voice that wants to take you by the hand and help you climb to higher levels. The saboteur is the voice that is making certain you do not thrive by holding you back, limiting your experiences, and denying your potential.

You'll regret what you ignored and let slip by more than what you went for and tried.

Be daring. Take risks. Live. Really Live. Matter. Love.

From your comfort zone, it will all be out of your grasp. Silence the fear so you can tune in to your inner voice. Listen to what the voice is saying and take a risk. If you want more Connection in your life, then be more loving; love is the glue that binds our connections. They aren't something you go out and get… Connection is something you recognize. We are all connected by the tapestry that is life. You simply need to remember, and *be* connected.

What doesn't work:

1. Making up painful stories in your head.
2. Ignoring your sexual preferences.
3. Blindly accepting any beliefs you have about sexuality.
4. Not communicating with sexual partners what you like and what you don't.
5. Setting unrealistic expectations of others.
6. Saying yes to people, places, and things that you really want to say no to.
7. Giving away your time without considering the consequences.
8. Allowing others to hold you emotionally hostage.
9. Holding onto people who want to be out of your life.
10. Making your love contingent on how much love you receive from others.
11. Living in the bubble of your Comfort Zone.

What does:

1. Rewriting your painful mental stories.
2. Recognizing your sexual/affectional orientation.
3. Exploring and determining your sexual likes and dislikes.
4. Questioning where your perception regarding sexuality came from and developing healthy, loving thoughts regarding your sexuality.
5. Exploring your body through self-stimulation.
6. Determining what you like and what you don't sexually, and communicating that clearly to sexual partners.
7. Developing healthy boundaries with people, places, and things to maintain your personal balance.
8. Valuing and protecting your time.
9. Putting past relationships in perspective.
10. Remembering, you are connected.
11. Living in love.
12. Stretching your Self beyond your Comfort Zone.

YOUR PERSONAL PLAN FOR CREATING A LIFETIME OF SELF–LOVE AND RESPECT

"It is good to have an end to journey toward; but it is the journey that matters, in the end." – Ursala K. La Guin

Let's pull together everything you've learned from the previous chapters to really begin *Choosing Me Now*. This chapter will help you solidify your plan to create the life you want in alignment with your Quality World. There are seven steps to this process:

1. Take personal inventory of where you are now.
2. Determine the areas you want to change.
3. Discover your "why."
4. Make a plan.
5. Create accountability.
6. Execute the plan.
7. Commit to continuous improvement.

STEP ONE: TAKE PERSONAL INVENTORY

"Patience is a form of wisdom. It demonstrates that we understand and accept the fact that sometimes things must unfold in their own time."
– Jon Kabat-Zinn

If your goal is to develop a more harmonious relationship with yourself, then it is important you're honest when assessing your current place in life. You may have the tendency either to be easy on yourself or to judge yourself harshly; remember, there is no one to be humble for, and there is no one to impress. This inventory is only about you—it's just yourself and your Self here. What do you have in your life that's working? What are the things you'd be better off letting go? If you tend to focus on those negative perceptions you have of yourself, I recommend you bask in the acknowledgment of the areas where you do well. Draw upon your strengths to make the changes you want to implement.

With this book in mind, ask yourself some questions; you may have already mastered some areas, but there may be some areas you would like to work on. The following inventory will help you decide where you want to begin.

WHO ARE YOU?

How well do you really know yourself? Do you love yourself? Are you ready to make changes if you don't? Would you want yourself as a friend? Have you identified and cleared out the messages you adopted that no longer serve you, if they ever actually did? Do you know where you start and others begin? Have you examined your values and beliefs and aligned your behavior with the things most important to you? Have you learned how to find the GLO in the painful experiences of your life?

Safety & Security: Are you in harmony with your relationship with money? Do you have deep appreciation for your body and its many functions? Are you respecting and maintaining your health?

Significance: Do you understand the importance of focusing on the one thing you can change—yourself? Do you recognize your inherent value and worth as a member of the human race? Have you identified, and are you working in, the area of your passion? Are you sharing your gifts with others?

Freedom: Do you have a harmonious relationship with your environment? Do you understand your role in your own misery and how to stop creating it? Are you free to be your Self?

Joy: Are you pleased with the level of Joy in your life? Do you have enough play? Are you able to deeply relax when the time is right? What is your relationship with learning? Who are your teachers and what are the life lessons you are currently learning?

Connection: Do you know how to give yourself physical pleasure? Are you aware of how your expectations can create challenges for you? Have you examined your thoughts and biases about love and how those values and beliefs help or hurt you from connecting with others and connecting with your Self?

Once you have answered these questions and completed an honest assessment of exactly where you stand, then it is time to choose what you want to let go of so you can make room for something better.

STEP TWO: DETERMINE THE AREAS YOU WANT TO CHANGE

"Letting go is not the same as giving up." – Tamara Star

Based on your personal inventory, there may be things you believe you would be better off giving up but, for some reason, you are holding on to them. This is a sign that it may be benefiting you somehow. You may need to experience some more pain before being ready to make the change. Welcome the pain, because it is a necessary step prior to change.

Understand that letting go isn't the same as giving up. You can want something in your life while understanding that, right now, letting go of that desire is in your best interest. That doesn't mean it won't come around again at a different time. You may not need to give it up forever, but just for now. When I was letting go of extra weight, something that helped me was letting go of my desire for chocolate right now. I would tell myself I could have it if I wanted it, but right then, I didn't want it.

Letting go of a friendship that isn't working may be the healthiest thing you can do. It doesn't mean you'll never be friends again, but just that, for right now, it's best to let go of the desire to be present and active in this person's life. Remember this anonymous quotation: "Just because it didn't last forever, doesn't mean it wasn't worth your while."

Letting go of a job that isn't working can open the path for a much better opportunity. It could come in the form of finding a job more suited to you, starting your own business, or possibly a fulfilling retirement.

When you decide to let go, you may experience pain, sadness, and frustration. This is part of the grieving process. Through this, it is important you develop acceptance and appreciation; being grateful for your current situation will allow you to release the negative quickly and with more ease than if you fight or dwell in it.

> *Pain* and *Frustration* from where you are today
> + *Acceptance* and *Appreciation* for it
> = The Possibility of Letting Go

Resisting reality, a negatively exhausting struggle, will keep you energetically tied to that situation, event, or person. Even if it's painful, learn to accept and appreciate the current situation for what it is teaching you, how it provides you a gift or an opportunity for something better.

Sometimes experiencing the opposite of what you want allows you to recognize what you *do* want when it shows up in your life. Despite the pain, the contrast may be necessary to illuminate what you really want. Welcome, accept, and appreciate this contrast. It is your friend.

One of my clients dated five women—all who displayed possessive, jealous behaviors—before he realized he wanted a partner who displays positive self-esteem. Another client learned how much loyalty was important to her when she discovered her husband had other lovers during their marriage. Another client needed pain in his joints to realize what he really wanted was to maintain a healthy lifestyle. Take a look at all the areas covered in this book and decide what things you want to change, make a list, then decide where you want to start.

You can start with the biggest change, believing that once

it's tackled the rest will be easier. Or, you can start small, and use the small victories to motivate you toward bigger changes. Identify one to five things you'd like to change. Choose changes that will stretch you without overwhelming you. If the change is huge, focus on it alone. Take on more if you want the challenge and variety of splitting your focus.

Whatever your approach, determine the areas in your life where you want to let go of what isn't working to make room for what will.

STEP THREE: DISCOVER YOUR "WHY"

"Letting go of what is already slipping away is how we actually enjoy our life." – Lewis Richmond

The things that aren't working in your life are sometimes things you are struggling to hold onto when they're trying to leave, such as a job that isn't a good fit or a lover that wants to end your relationship. If you pay attention to synchronicity in your life, you may notice there are signs pointing you in the direction you are meant to take.

I have a client who isn't happy with her job. She loves the work, but hates the politics of her office. Because of this, she's been considering starting her own business. Whenever I speak to her, there is something new irritating her. She recognizes these are little nudges moving her toward starting her own business, and though she's not ignoring them, she's not ready to pull the trigger just yet. The job is "slipping away" but she is still holding on. It's okay to hold on to increase the pain and frustration, but don't keep yourself in that state forever. Staying too long may trick you into believing you're stuck in the job, with the extra weight, or in the relationship. You'll hold on for dear life in fear of what might happen if you let go, but letting go is how you begin to live.

Think about the areas you want to change and ask yourself why. Why do you want to let go? What are you trying to make room for? What will replace the things you want to let go of? Why do you want that? Why is it important to you? How will your life improve? These questions are designed to help you comprehend your "why."

If you don't have a meaningful "why," when things become difficult, you will be tempted to return to your former behavior. Having a significant reason for this change will help you stay the course when things get challenging. You will want to get crystal clear about your reason, write it down, and remind yourself often.

Step Four: Make a Plan

"You are not what life hands to you, you are the life you make." – Rachel Roy

You've made an assessment, decided what you want to change, and have identified your reason. Now it's time to make a plan.

My good friend, Karen ODonnell, does a workshop about following the path that opens up before you. She coaches people to recognize signs—doors closing, windows opening, opportunities presenting themselves—and taking the path that reveals itself. Trust in the Universe to deliver exactly what you need when you need it.

In this process, there is one caveat. When you are on your path and relax into the journey, things often seem to effortlessly fall into place. However, when perched on the precipice of success, the Law of Opposites may appear to challenge your resolve. It presents you with all the things you don't want while pursuing the things you do. When the Law of Opposites comes into play, you need to recognize it and persevere.

It takes many forms: a major life event, subconscious sabotage, or the offering of a compromise to keep you in your current circumstances. Having a plan in place can help you push through this natural resistance. However, if you find the entire journey is fraught with obstacles and resistance, then you may want to evaluate whether or not this path is actually for you. We sometimes have tunnel vision and spend a lot of time trying to force that square peg into the round hole. For me, this occurs when I pursue something someone else thinks I should, or I doubt my natural path is valid and I try a different road for the sake of convenience or ease. Every step I take in the direction that isn't meant for me feels as though I'm trekking through mud. There seems to be forces holding me back, impeding my progress.

You will need to be careful when determining whether the resistance you experience occurs all along the path or as you approach the realization of your goals. With the former, you may want to reevaluate your path. With the latter, you will want to push through to the goal.

Record your plan, whether it's in a journal, an audio file, video, or a typed document on your computer. Make that commitment.

The elements of a good plan include the following:

- Simplicity—The plan should state what you will do in simple terms. There is no need to make it convoluted.
- Attainability—The plan should stretch you but not be so difficult you will fail.
- Measurement Criteria—There should be an objective way to measure your process.
- Specificity—There should be enough detail so you cannot makes excuses for not doing what you have planned.
- Repetition—The plan needs to be something you will do over and over, preferably each day, to create new habits.
- Immediacy—The plan should start immediately, not at some point in the future.
- Target Dates—Be sure to include the date by when you expect to complete each step of the plan.
- Non-contingency—Non-contingency means you are in full control of the implementation of the plan. When you have a plan that is dependent upon other people, your plan can be sabotaged through no fault of your own.
- Positivity—Many people write plans about what

they are going to *stop* doing but fail to record what they plan to replace that with. A positive plan delineates both what you are going to stop doing as well as what you intend to do instead.

• Follow up—Every good plan includes a system for following up. The plan and progress made needs to be reviewed periodically.

BONUS: Each plan should address the concerns about what could get in the way of, or sabotage, the execution of the plan and how those potential obstacles will be overcome.

Once the plan has been created, it's time to think about what system you will put in place to increase accountability.

STEP FIVE: CREATE ACCOUNTABILITY

"Accountability breeds response-ability." –Stephen Covey

When your motivation wanes, accountability is the process that helps you stay on track. When I get serious about writing a book, I tell people about it. When I want to lose weight, I make sure other people know, and I get a workout partner. When I'm trying to develop a new habit to replace one I want to let go, I make sure others know. I'm vocal about my goals so others will hold me accountable. Letting at least one other person in on what you're trying to accomplish may help you make progress when you otherwise might procrastinate.

When I'm unsure or not ready, I don't want to be held accountable, so I tell no one. I want to be able to abort at any time without the embarrassment of others knowing I didn't follow through.

Another thing to consider is having the "right" person in charge of holding you accountable. Naturally, at the end of the day, you are the only one responsible for your success or failure, but choosing the right accountability partner can improve your odds.

If you want to get physically fit, it makes sense to choose a partner in better or roughly the same shape as you who is equally committed to the goal. Choosing someone with no interest in improving their health may have the best intentions, but could have a subconscious desire to see you stay exactly as you are so you will both be in the same set of circumstances.

You may decide to improve yourself financially and reduce your debt. If you choose an accountability partner in more debt than you, he or she may not want you to climb out of debt because you will leave them in your dust.

Suppose you want a promotion at work and your husband agrees to hold you accountable. However, he's worried your promotion will mean you will be home less often and his needs might be neglected.

In every one of these examples, you have not chosen the best accountability partner. When choosing, ask yourself, "Is this person as committed to my success as I am? Does this person have a vested interest in keeping me exactly where I am?" If you can't say yes to the first question and no to the second, then choose someone else.

If there are no family or friends who can provide the accountability you need, you may consider hiring someone. It's common for a person to hire a personal trainer when they get serious about releasing excess weight. Why not hire a personal coach when you are serious about making lifestyle changes? An objective coach has no personal agenda other than supporting his or her clients to accomplish the goals they set—that's what I call an excellent accountability partner.

If you have five areas you want to let go of to create room for something better, you may require five different accountability partners. You want to find the right fit based on their strengths and your particular goals. Who will you invite to join you on this journey?

Once you have your accountability partners in place, it's time to execute your plan.

STEP SIX: EXECUTE THE PLAN

"We begin to find and become ourselves when we notice how we are already found, already truly, entirely, wildly, messily, marvelously who we were born to be." – Anne Lamott

Flexibility, resilience, and balance are three important characteristics to strengthen and rely on as you execute your plan.

FLEXIBILITY

When beginning any long-term endeavor, it is vital you remember to remain flexible. Becoming rigid about what you want to accomplish and how you will accomplish it can cause you to miss a number of excellent opportunities along the way.

Some of my most amazing opportunities thus far have been detours I came upon while on my path, implementing my plan. Detours can be of the derailing or opportunistic variety. Ask yourself, "Is this detour in line with my values?" When it isn't, classify it as a derailing detour and avoid it. If it is, be flexible and consider seeing where the detour leads. While working on my coaching and training business, I have welcomed a number of detour opportunities: developing a twenty-five hour curriculum for court-mandated parenting classes, serving as an expert for divorce services in Croatia, writing a book on diversity, becoming a book coach, and creating a BCC-approved coaching program. I did not pursue any of these opportunities, but I noticed these detours on my path; considered their alignment with my vision, mission, and values; and said yes to them all at different times in my career. All added value and led to other wonderful opportunities. Some of the detours I said no to were teaching classes at the university level, being a group coach, and learning to create websites. I won't know if these were missed opportunities because I didn't take them; they weren't in line with my mission of helping people get along better with the important people in their lives, including themselves. I have no regrets and believe staying my course in those situations was the right decision.

When you need to make adjustments to your plan, flexibility is necessary. As you execute your original plan, you may find a different, more feasible path to success. When what you are doing isn't working to reach your goal, be flexible enough to adjust your course.

In the creation and execution of your plan, remain flexible enough to modify your direction and explore detours along the way.

RESILIENCE

Resilience is defined by *Merriam-Webster Dictionary* as the "ability to recover from or adjust easily to misfortune or change." Since change is the only thing that you can be sure of, resilience is a wonderful ability to possess and develop. Resilience is like a muscle; you need to exercise it properly in order for it to grow.

Change is going to happen, and you will experience challenges. The ability to adapt will be of great assistance in the execution of your plan. Resilience depends on your mental and physical health, as you will need the stamina to weather stress and the emotional mindset to view adversity as a challenge instead of an obstacle.

The following is a list of thoughts you can think to exercise your resiliency muscle:

- I may have made an error, but I sure learned a lot.
- Yes, I've had some difficulties in my life, but I'm still here.
- When something bad happens, I can always find the good in it.
- I know change happens, and I don't always love it, but I can roll with it.
- Even though there may be challenges along the way, things work out for me in the end.
- Life isn't always fair, but I know how to make the best of what I have.
- No matter what happens in my life, there is always

much to be grateful for.
- This may seem horrible now, but I know when I look back on it, it won't seem so bad.
- I have the resources I need to get through this challenge.
- I may have to let go of something important, but it will create room for something even better.

Some of *The Resilience Mindset* may come naturally to you. If it does, then check off resiliency as one of your strengths. However, if it doesn't come easy, then be on the lookout for opportunities to flex your resilience muscle. Use the statements of *The Resilience Mindset* or create your own to help you strengthen your resilience. Remember to also maintain your physical strength as this is an important factor in being able to carry out *The Resilience Mindset*.

Being resilient will prevent you from stopping dead in your tracks when things do not go according to plan, because they won't always. You will stop, assess, regroup, re-plan and move forward.

BALANCE

Maintaining balance during your plan's execution is also vitally important. As stated earlier, there is nothing you can do to disrupt the balance of the Universe, but you can disrupt your own personal balance. However, it is best to ensure natural balance remains intact, because it's easier to maintain balance than to restore balance.

There are several areas in your life where balance is crucial to your well-being; maintaining balance in all areas of your life is incredibly challenging, but something worth aspiring to.

Trusting in universal balance helps to maintain personal balance. When you know there is nothing you can do to disrupt overall balance in the world, you are free to focus on the one thing you can control—your personal balance.

As you work to maintain balance in your own life, here

are the areas you might attend to. Keep in mind, people have their own optimal point of balance in these categories:

Balance safety and calculated risks: Depending on the strength of your Safety & Security need, you may want to increase either your safety or your risk-taking. What is it you need for balance? Are you just right, playing it too safe or taking too many risks?

Balance spending and saving: Depending on the strength of your need for Safety & Security, you may want to increase or decrease your spending and increase or decrease your savings. Do you find you have just the precise balance between these two extremes, or would you benefit from spending more/saving less or saving more/spending less?

Balance movement and stillness: Maintaining balance can be tricky. You know exercise is important for your overall health, and yet spiritually, it's also important to be still to connect with your Higher Power. Balancing these may seem contradictory, but it isn't—you need both. Do you have the right amount of movement and exercise, or do you need more or less? Are you making time to be still, or do you need more or less stillness in your life?

Balance productivity and relaxation: A healthy balance between productivity and relaxation will serve you well. The interaction between your needs for Significance and Joy will determine your best balance point here. If you find Joy in your productivity, then balance tends to occur automatically, but take a close look to see if you need a bit more relaxation. When your need for Joy is high, you might be looking for less productivity and more relaxation. If it's Significance that's high, then you may be craving more productivity to experience the balance you crave. Are you balanced here, or do you need more productivity/less relaxation or more relaxation/less productivity?

Balance humility and confidence: There is a fine line to walk between confidence and arrogance. When you cross over into arrogance, the balance of the Universe tends to show up to let you know you aren't at its center. To be humble means you recognize that you are only acting through your divinely given gifts, so you are nothing special. Don't let humility contradict the value of your Self; you also need to recognize your value in using your gifts to serve others. Assess your balance in this area—are you too humble, too confident, or well-balanced on this continuum?

Balance freedom and responsibility: Experiencing balance here means you exercise your freedom while accepting the responsibility that comes with it. There are some who will do whatever they want and try to deny the resulting consequences. On the other end, there are people who will accept responsibility not only for their own choices, but also for the choices of others. This is taking too much responsibility. Where do you fall? Are you balanced here? Do you exercise so much freedom you are hurting others? Or do you accept more than your share of responsibility and, ultimately, hurt yourself?

Balance love of self and love of others: Are you loving yourself most, others most, or both equally? Depending on how high your Connection need is, you may attend to others' needs before your own, or you may exclusively attend to your own to the detriment of others. This book is essentially about choosing yourself first because, unless you do, you will be no good to help others. However, the strength of your Connection need may not allow you to always choose yourself over others. There will be times when choosing others is the very thing that meets your need for Connection, as long as you are not doing it with resentment. What is your balancing point? Are you balanced, do you need to love yourself more, or do you need to take a look at loving others more?

Balance giving and receiving: It's the Law of Reciprocity that speaks to giving and receiving. Universal balance tells us there are those in balance on this factor, and there are others who are either predominantly givers or receivers, thus creating the overall balance. When you have a higher need for Connection, you may more likely be a giver. If you have a higher need for Safety & Security or Significance, it is more likely you're a taker. It's also possible that you use a behavior of giving or receiving to satisfy a need. For example, if you find you are low in Connection, then you may think taking will best provide it. If you are lower in Significance, you may try to get that met through giving. Where is your perfect balance in this area? Are you there, or do you need to give more or take more?

Balance negativity and positivity: As discussed earlier, your brain is hardwired for negativity, so you need to train it to notice the positives, even in difficult situations. They are there; you just need to uncover them. If you are someone always basking in positivity, then in order to find balance, you may need to begin looking for the tradeoffs in every situation as they are also there. Being able to see the Universal balance of equal positive and negative in every situation will help neutralize the emotionality and allow you to make a reasoned assessment.

Balance pain with gratitude: I have not yet discovered a way to get through life without some degree of pain. However, I've come to realize that perhaps I wouldn't want to since there are so many benefits from finding gratitude through the pain. It's painful when the real world doesn't match your Quality World, but immediately after experiencing that painful perception, you can shift your focus to gratitude. Always seek the GLO—gift, lesson, or opportunity—in every painful situation. Holding onto pain may cause you to forget about gratitude completely; you may need to experience a bit more pain in your current situation to provide you with the incentive to change it. Where are you on this factor? Are you balanced, or do you need more pain or more gratitude?

Seeking balance in all things while you are executing your plan will provide you the strength you need to carry on. Whenever you find yourself at a standstill, assess your balance and make the necessary corrections.

STEP SEVEN: COMMIT TO CONTINUOUS IMPROVEMENT

"You have the ability to reinvent yourself endlessly. That's your beauty."
– Lidia Yuknavitch

I hope you've committed to making a plan to create what works for you by letting go of what doesn't. That's terrific!

Quality is always a moving target; once you believe you've reached it, another goal may appear that will improve that quality. Self-improvement is a process that never ends. What you currently envision as your best Self may pale in comparison to the best Self you can see once you have let go of the things that aren't working. As you invite the things that will work better into your life, your vision of your Self will grow bigger and more defined.

When you accomplish the goals you set today, be ready to set new goals when you arrive there. You will constantly evolve to higher aspirations when you are committed to continuous improvement. You are either growing or dying; waxing or waning. Which are you doing?

As you move closer to your Ideal Self, you will see the quality of your time, experiences, and relationships improve. You will meet influencers and helpers along the way who will connect, support, and encourage you as you let go of people who are not working for you. As you align your time and activities to match your values, you will see those things working better for you. Your time will have more meaning, resulting in richer experiences.

As you are inspired, you will aspire to go higher, not just for your own glory or advancement, but for the good of those you serve. As you ascend to a higher plane, look for new teachers and mentors along the way. As your vibrational energy increases, you will attract those who vibrate at your same level. Everyone you come in contact with has the potential to become your teacher. Some people will teach you what you want to do and how you want be, while others will show you what you don't want to do and how you don't want to be. Both lessons are equally valid.

Watch for people placed in your life who will help you reach your goals, possibly through their connections, their knowledge, or their experience. Watch for people who are already successful at what you are attempting to do. They will have much to teach you. Tap into those resources.

Choosing Me Now has been a vehicle for me to create

the kind of relationship I want with myself. As I explored different aspects of my personality, got to know myself better, and assessed what was working and what wasn't, I wrote down my path for you to follow, if you choose. Your path is unique and will need to be specifically tailored to suit your personality and aspirations. It is my sincere hope that you have found a new or improved path for yourself within these pages.

I wish for you the ability to love yourself as much as you love others, the willingness to put your own well-being first in your life, and the openness to allow Divine flow into your life as you let go of what doesn't work to make room for what does. There is no limit to what can happen when you do!

What doesn't work:

1. Being unaware about yourself and the effect you have on others.
2. Focusing on what is wrong in your life.
3. Getting stuck in the grieving process.
4. Resisting reality.
5. Making plans to change without understanding why you want to.
6. Making plans without attending to the specifics listed on page 203.
7. Functioning with no attention to balance.
8. Attempting major change without any accountability.

What does:

1. Taking assessment of where you are now.
2. Being honest with yourself.
3. Focusing on what is right in your life.
4. Determining the areas you want to change.
5. Balancing the pain with the benefits.
6. Discovering a meaningful reason for letting go.
7. Making a plan that includes the specifics beginning on page 203.
8. Striving for internal balance.
9. Creating accountability.
10. Executing the plan.
11. Committing to continuous improvement.
12. Remaining teachable.

If you enjoyed this book and found it helpful, I would deeply appreciate a moment of your time to leave a review. This way, other readers who could benefit from this information will have a better chance of finding it. *Choosing Me Now* is listed on both Amazon and Goodreads, so either site will accept a review.

Thanks for reading! I hope you're confident with your new set of tools to start choosing *you* now.

– *Kim Olver*

CPSIA information can be obtained
at www.ICGtesting.com
Printed in the USA
FFOW03n1500031017
40477FF